One Body in Christ

ONE BODY IN CHRIST

Ecumenical Snapshots

Owen F. Cummings

Foreword by
Seymour Baker House

◦PICKWICK Publications • Eugene, Oregon

ONE BODY IN CHRIST
Ecumenical Snapshots

Copyright © 2015 Owen F. Cummings. All rights reserved. Except for brief quotations in critical publications or reviews, no part of this book may be reproduced in any manner without prior written permission from the publisher. Write: Permissions. Wipf and Stock Publishers, 199 W. 8th Ave., Suite 3, Eugene, OR 97401.

Pickwick Publications
An Imprint of Wipf and Stock Publishers
199 W. 8th Ave., Suite 3
Eugene, OR 97401

www.wipfandstock.com

ISBN 13: 978-1-4982-0215-2

Cataloguing-in-Publication Data

Cummings, Owen F.

    One body in Christ : ecumenical snapshots / Owen F. Cummings

    xiv + 120 p. ; 23 cm. Includes bibliographical references.

    ISBN 13: 978-1-4982-0215-2

    1. Church. I. Title.

BX1746 C86 2015

Manufactured in the U.S.A.

Dedicated to:

Matthew

Michael

Natalia

Finley

Cora

Maeve,

the next generation.

Contents

Foreword by Seymour Baker House | ix
Introduction | xi

1   John Wesley's Letter to a Roman Catholic | 1
2   Bishop Lesslie Newbigin's *The Household of God* | 9
3   Vatican II, Decree on Ecumenism | 24
4   Ecumenical Pioneer, Michael Hurley, SJ (1923–2011) | 40
5   John Macquarrie, Church, and Ecumenism | 53
6   Avery Dulles, SJ, *Models of the Church* | 70
7   Frances M. Young on Theology, Mary, and Prayer | 82
8   Eucharist, Ecumenism, and George Hunsinger | 95

Conclusion | 112
Bibliography | 115

Foreword

In Owen Cummings's inspiring collection of "ecumenical snapshots" we discover Jesuits, Methodists, Presbyterians, Anglicans, and a Catholic conciliar Decree on Ecumenism urgently inviting us to recognize that what unites us as Christians is far stronger than what divides us, the "experienced presence and action of God" in ourselves and one another. From an assuredly vast periodic table of theological elements, Cummings selects as examples disparate voices, some well-known, others happy discoveries, to suggest the range of resources available when constructing an ecumenical universe. How encouraging it is to find Michael Hurley, SJ—whose Archbishop opposed his efforts to help heal Ireland's sectarian violence—presented alongside John Wesley and his conviction that we can only build our relationship with God through our relationship with neighbor. Here also we need two theologians who explore the nature of the church in a pluralist and relativist world—Lesslie Newbigin, the renowned missionary bishop whose career took him between England and the Indian sub-continent, and Avery Dulles, SJ, whose work illuminates his conviction that the Gospel cannot inhere in us without itself being incarnated in human culture. And finally, John Macquarrie, Frances Young, and George Hunsinger, three pioneers in contemporary ecumenical ecclesiology, draw us out of our sectarian and epistemological divides into the prior claims of our shared Christian identity. As Dulles reminds us, models matter, and models of the church can inhibit as well as encourage our ability to change. Animated by an understanding that ecumenism is fundamentally a matter of the heart, even as doctrinal consensus is growing, Cummings gives us every reason to be optimistic that ecumenical formation is possible. And indeed, if we are listening closely to the gospel and the exemplars he presents here, nearer to us than we think.

—Seymour Baker House
Professor of Church History
Mount Angel Seminary

Introduction

The image of snapshots in the title for this little book on ecclesiology needs some explanation. This book is not an introduction to ecclesiology, nor is it a "video" laying out a panoramic and systematic theology of the church. Rather, it is a series of reflections, or "snapshots," on the church. We are looking at the church through a series of individual snapshots of significant thinkers who have contributed to our understanding of church, as well as to one event, Vatican II (1962–65) and its Decree on Ecumenism.

Ecclesial snapshots are also necessarily ecumenical snapshots. To paraphrase a famous line from John Donne, "No church is an island entire of itself." For Roman Catholics this has been the case since Vatican II. From Edinburgh 1910 and its World Missionary Conference to Amsterdam in 1948 and the inauguration of the World Council of Churches, to Vatican II's Decree on Ecumenism, church unity is an intrinsic part of all mainline approaches to theology and especially to ecclesiology.

It seems to me that one way of developing ecumenical-ecclesiology is through these ecclesial snapshots. There is much to be said for engaging specific ideas of individual theologians, cumulatively heading towards a more comprehensive understanding of the church. This might be compared to Aidan Nichols, OP's recent book, *Figuring Out the Church, Her Marks, and Her Masters*.[1] Nichols deals with individual Roman Catholic thinkers—Henri de Lubac, Jean Tillard, Hans Urs von Balthasar, and Charles Journet—whereas this book deals with other Christians as well as Catholics. Here we begin with the eighteenth century: John Wesley's 1749 *Letter to a Roman Catholic*. This is followed in chapter 2 with an account of Lesslie Newbigin's *Household of God*. Coming shortly after the inauguration of the World Council of Churches in 1948, Newbigin offers a remarkably

---

1. Nichols, OP, *Figuring Out the Church*.

INTRODUCTION

balanced ecumenical ecclesiology. The Decree on Ecumenism from Vatican II brought the Catholic Church into the mainstream of the ecumenical movement. This decree remains a powerful statement even now, fifty years and more after its promulgation. Vatican II was the catalyst for all kinds of ecumenical engagement. In an Ireland torn by violence, some of whose roots included Catholic and Protestant sectarian divisions, the Irish Jesuit Michael Hurley was a pioneering ecumenical force. His *Theology of Ecumenism* remains as valuable today as it was when he published it in 1969. The ecumenical movement and ecclesiological reflection may have gone some distance since then, but Hurley's principles still seem sound and attractive. John Macquarrie is the focus of chapter 5. Macquarrie, one of the ablest Anglican systematic theologians of the twentieth century, most probably heard Lesslie Newbigin's *Household of God* when it was delivered as the Kerr Lectures in the Faculty of Divinity of the University of Glasgow. Macquarrie was working on his PhD at the time, and though his research focused on the connections between Heidegger and Bultmann, as a minister of the church he undoubtedly had an interest in ecclesiology. In chapter 6 we turn to the eminent Catholic ecclesiologist and ecumenist Avery Dulles, SJ. While Macquarrie probably heard Newbigin's lectures on ecclesiology Glasgow, he definitely heard Dulles's Martin D'Arcy lectures at Oxford University in 1983. Macquarrie was Lady Margaret Professor of Divinity in Oxford. Dulles's *Catholicity*—the D'Arcy lectures in published form—was a fitting sequel to his better-known *Models of the Church*, and it is to the latter that we shall turn in this sixth chapter.[2] Chapters 7 and 8 are focused on the Methodist theologian Frances M. Young, and on the ecumenical approach to the Eucharist through the contribution of Presbyterian theologian George Hunsinger.

My hope is that this book makes some small contribution to keeping the ecumenical flame alive for all committed Christians, especially at a time when it seems not to be burning so brightly. There is a need especially for what has been called "receptive ecumenism." This is an understanding of ecumenism as properly "a matter of the heart before it is a matter of the head; a matter of falling in love with the experienced presence and action of God in the people, practices, even structures of another tradition and being impelled thereby to search for ways in which all impediments to closer relationship might be overcome."[3] Perhaps the brief reflections in this book

2. Dulles, SJ, *The Catholicity of the Church*.
3. Murray, "Receptive Ecumenism and Catholic Learning—Establishing the Agenda," 15.

Introduction

will help Christians of different traditions not only move towards a more informed perspective intellectually about each other, but also towards a greater love for each other as together we witness to the good news of the gospel of Jesus Christ.

1

John Wesley's Letter to a Roman Catholic

If we cannot as yet think alike in all things, at least we may love alike. Herein we cannot possibly do amiss. For of one point none can doubt a moment: God is love; and he that dwelleth in love, dwelleth in God, and God in him.

JOHN WESLEY.[1]

Introduction

The Irish Jesuit theologian and ecumenist Michael Hurley was an "accredited visitor" to the World Methodist Conference in London in 1966. Over the years Hurley was to develop a great love for the Methodist tradition, but it was at this conference that it began. In the course of the proceedings he heard reference made by Stanley Worrall, an Irish delegate to the conference, to John Wesley's "Letter to a Roman Catholic," written from Dublin in 1749. Stanley Worrall, at the time living and working in Belfast in Northern Ireland, was no naïve ecumenist. Worrall wrote *a propos* of this conference in 1966: "The love for Rome is not so great everywhere as it appears to be in this chamber. I do not share the prejudice, but it exists in many places

---

1. Hurley, ed., *John Wesley's Letter*, 56.

in the world and among many of our own people, who still believe that the Roman Catholic Church is not part of the Christian body, but is an insidious conspiracy of the devil."[2]

Returning home after this experience, Hurley sought out a copy of Wesley's letter to which reference had been made by Worrall. He published a new edition of the letter accompanied by his own introduction. As a result of editing John Wesley's letter, Hurley was appointed to the World Methodist Council/Roman Catholic Church Joint Commission. Hurley writes of his experience: "Membership of the Commission broadened our horizons not only geographically but also spiritually. One thing became immediately obvious: neither side was a monolith."[3]

Hurley's reason for writing an introduction to John Wesley's letter was to provide readers who were not Methodists with some basic information about Wesley and some background to the letter. Immediately, Hurley recognized the differences between John Wesley himself and today's Methodists. "They differ from him chiefly because, whereas he was and always remained a practicing member of the Church of England—an Anglican as we would say—they are not. Unlike him they are members of a distinct and separate world-wide communion in one or other of its many independent Churches with their own system of Church order and government, their own ordained clergy to administer the sacraments, their own more or less different outlook in matters of worship and doctrine."[4] Nonetheless, Hurley quite rightly points out that not only are contemporary Methodists attached historically and devotionally to John Wesley, but also they recognize as important Wesley's *Notes on the New Testament* as well as the first four volumes of his *Sermons*. Hurley goes on to make a singularly important point. In view of the fact that Wesley wished to establish a religious society *within* the church, and not something alongside the church or outside the church in some fashion, his religious society bears a strong family resemblance to the religious orders within the Catholic Church—the Franciscans, the Dominicans, the Jesuits, etc. The evangelizing projects of these societies within the church were intended to make the church at large better what it was called to be. And so with John Wesley. He set out to make the church of his time better what it was called to be. He did not wish to be ecclesiologically a separatist. His movement was to be a reforming, missionary, and revivalist

2. In *Methodist Recorder*, September 1, 1966, 4.
3. Hurley, *Healing and Hope*, 56.
4. Hurley, ed., *John Wesley's Letter*, 22.

movement *within* the church. "Wesley certainly provided a reforming and missionary agency by means of which a deep and widespread religious revival took place in Great Britain and Ireland, and in America such a rapid expansion of Christianity as 'had not been equaled in Christendom since the Apostolic Era.'"[5] Behind Wesley's Methodism lay a high spirituality with an evangelical simplicity. Central to this high spirituality and to Wesley's revivalism was a strong sacramental and eucharistic focus. His desire was that his disciples attend their own Anglican parish churches to celebrate the Eucharist.[6]

Sometimes Wesley is judged to be indifferent to doctrine and theology. The great American Methodist theologian Albert Outler regarded this judgment as "mildly outrageous."[7] Something of that judgment has stuck, however, and it may have to do with Wesley's time. He was more interested in what today might be called "spirituality" rather than in the so many forms of controversial theology that were current. Wesley was far from indifferent to orthodox theology and Christianity, but he saw these as serving holiness of life.

John Wesley's Letter to a Roman Catholic

The *Letter to a Roman Catholic* was written from Dublin, Ireland on July 18, 1749. Wesley had arrived in Ireland in April of that year and had been busy evangelizing and preaching throughout the country. He arrived in Dublin in July and spent two weeks both preaching and writing. He writes well of the Irish, "For natural sweetness of temper, for courtesy and hospitality, I have never seen any people like the Irish," but he also had at times a decidedly negative and hostile attitude to Irish Catholics: "I was surprised to find how little the Irish Papists are changed in a hundred years. Most of them retain the same bitterness, yea, and thirst for blood, as ever, and would as freely now cut the throats of all the Protestants as they did in the last century."[8] Undoubtedly, such sentiments reflect the hostile response he encountered in various parts of the country, especially in Cork, but it is important to recognize also that the times were different and the hostility may

---

5. Ibid., 23–24.
6. For a brief sense of Wesley's eucharistic discipline and theology, see Cummings, *Eucharistic Doctors*, 215–25.
7. Outler, ed., *John Wesley*, 28.
8. Hurley, ed., *John Wesley's Letter*, 33.

not have been particularly religious as much as it was political. In respect of the violence to which Wesley refers Michael Hurley reminds us: "We must remember that cruelty and brutality were common in the everyday life of this period and in particular that violence was a general feature of the age, its perpetrators as well as its victims belonging to no one class or creed."[9]

While Hurley seems right in regarding Wesley's *Letter* as an open letter and not addressed to any one particular individual, he also surmises that it may have been influenced by a booklet published in 1749 by George Berkeley, Anglican Bishop of Cloyne and a philosopher. Berkeley's booklet had three editions and was entitled *A Word to the Wise: Or, An Exhortation by a Member of the Established Church to the Roman Catholic Clergy of Ireland*. The booklet begins with the following words, words reminiscent of the irenic attitude of Wesley in his *Letter*: "Be not startled, Reverend Sirs, to find yourselves addressed by one of a different Communion. We are indeed (to our shame be it spoken) more inclined to hate for those articles wherein we differ, than to love one another for those wherein we agree. But, if we cannot extinguish, let us at least suspend our animosities, and, forgetting our religious feuds, consider ourselves in the amiable light of countrymen and neighbors. . . . Why, then, should we not conspire in one and the same design—to promote the common good of our country."[10] It now appears to be the case that Berkeley's book was not published until October 1749, months after Wesley's *Letter*.[11] There is, therefore, no possible influence of Berkeley on Wesley in this regard. But what is surely interesting, perhaps even more interesting, is the irenic tone of both texts. George Berkeley and John Wesley were not only not pouring vitriol on Irish Roman Catholics, but they were also looking to their good, both temporal and spiritual.

Now we come to the letter itself. Wesley begins by acknowledging the hurt and anger on both sides, Catholic and Protestant. "We are on both sides less willing to help one another, and more ready to hurt each other. Hence brotherly love is utterly destroyed; and each side, looking on the other as monsters, gives way to anger, hatred, malice, to every unkind affection, which have frequently broke out in such inhuman barbarities as

---

9. Ibid., 35.

10. Cited in Hurley, ed., *John Wesley's Letter*, 42–43.

11. On page 44 Hurley notes the research done on this point by John Brady, SJ, one of his former students, and the upshot of the research is to establish definitively the October date for Berkeley's publication.

are scarce named among the heathens."[12] Wesley may be referring to some of his experiences in his evangelizing expeditions throughout Ireland, but he surely is also referring to the enmities that had grown between the people of the Reformation and Catholic traditions, the hostilities, and especially the controversial theologies that were developed against each other. That leads Wesley to comment "Now, can nothing be done, even allowing us on both sides to retain their own opinions, for the softening our hearts towards each other, the giving a check to this flood of unkindness, and restoring at least some small degree of love among our neighbors and countrymen?"[13] In this sentence he clearly recognizes the differences that theology makes—"retain[ing] . . . own opinions"—but he asks about, far more importantly, "the softening our hearts towards each other . . . ." What a wonderful phrase that is, and how very contemporary, "softening our hearts towards each other"!

At this point in the *Letter* Wesley goes on to provide a fine summary of the Creed, a summary that would be acceptable to any Catholic, and so he asks rhetorically: "Now, is there anything wrong in this? Is there any one point which you do not believe as well as we?" Needless to say, of course, he acknowledges that there is more to Christian belief in its various traditions than the Creed alone. "But you think we ought to believe more. We will not now enter into the dispute. Only let me ask, if a man sincerely believes thus much, and practices accordingly, can anyone possibly persuade you to think that such a man shall perish everlastingly?"[14] Having emphasized that the practice of Christian faith in ordinary life is every bit as important as its profession in the Creed, he recognized that this is no less central for Roman Catholics.

Wesley knows full well that there are differences, and indeed serious differences between Catholic and Protestant forms of worship and he makes two points about these differences. First, he insists to Catholics that "I am not persuading you to leave or change your religion, but to follow after that fear and love of God without which all religion is vain." There is no cheap proselytism in Wesley's perspective. Second, he emphasizes that all authentic worship must be "worship . . . in spirit and in truth, with your heart as well as your lips, with your spirit and with your understanding

---

12. Hurley, ed., *John Wesley's Letter*, 48.
13. Ibid.
14. Ibid., 52.

also." Going through rituals mechanically for either Catholic or Protestant is not enough. One must worship "with one's heart as well as one's lips."

Having considered both the Creed and worship, Wesley now goes on to provide an account of the Christian moral life. He does this by working his way through the Ten Commandments. There is a very contemporary ring to the way he sets about this in the *Letter*. These three sections of the *Letter* parallel the first three sections of the 1994 *Catechism of the Catholic Church*—the Creed, liturgy or worship, the moral life. Wesley is expecting no disagreement with his articulation of Christian faith, nor should there be on the part of Catholics. Catholics may wish to say more, but that ought not to detract from this broad swathe of agreement in faith.

The final part of Wesley's *Letter* is beautifully ecumenical and worthy of more extensive quotation.

> Are we not thus far agreed? Let us thank God for this, and receive it as a fresh token of his love. But if God still loveth us, we ought also to love one another. We ought, without this endless jangling about opinions, to provoke one another to love and to good works. Let the points wherein we differ stand aside: here are enough wherein we agree, enough be the ground of every Christian temper and of every Christian action. . . . In the name, then, and in the strength of God, let us resolve, first, not to hurt one another; to do nothing unkind or unfriendly to each other, nothing which we would not have done to ourselves. Rather let us endeavor after every instance of a kind, friendly and Christian behavior towards each other. Let us resolve, secondly, God being our helper, to speak nothing harsh or unkind of each other, . . . to use only the language of love, to speak with all softness and tenderness, with the most endearing expression which is consistent with truth and sincerity. Let us, thirdly, resolve to harbor no unkind thought, no unfriendly temper towards each other. . . . Let us, fourthly, endeavor to help each other on in whatever we are agreed leads to the Kingdom.[15]

There are other aspects of Wesley's attitude to Catholicism that are less irenic. For example, he was suspicious of the political views of Catholics, especially in relation to the English Crown. He also found the Catholic veneration of images to be a profound error.[16] That was over two and a half centuries ago. Since Vatican II theological dialogue between Catholicism and Methodism has continued to grow. It needs to be pointed out, however, that

---

15. Ibid., 55–56.
16. See Wainwright, "Catholics and Methodists," 39.

so much still needs to be done to build relationships between Methodists and Catholics. It is sadly but well put by Methodist theologian Geoffrey Wainwright: "In all honesty, however, we should have to admit that those two and a half centuries (from the time of Wesley's letter) contained long periods of silence on account of mutual ignorance as well as some sharp bursts of express mutual dismissal and polemics."[17]

Conclusion

Bishop Richard Challoner (1691–1781) was an English Roman Catholic contemporary of John Wesley. He was the author of many books, some devotional and some controversial, and an ardent pastor of souls. Exactly the same may be said of John Wesley (1703–91). The ministry of both men had so very much in common. They were both on fire with the love of God and with love for people. That is why Methodist historian and theologian David Butler ends his book *Methodists and Papists* with these words:

> I like to think that when John Wesley died in 1791 he found himself in the same heaven as Richard Challoner who had gone there some ten years before. As polite men they will have initially regretted that they never met and apologized for their misrepresentations of each other's positions. But it will be bliss for them to be speaking the same language and answering the same praises of the God who was utterly real for both of them on earth and is now seen face to face.[18]

Butler's vision of this heavenly encounter between Richard Challoner and John Wesley is very welcome in our times. In some quarters it has become popular to speak of "the winter of ecumenism." Working in the area of ecumenism often brings frustration and heartache in its wake. It is so difficult to measure success, since there is uncertainty about what success, especially in its institutional mode, might look like. The words of Jesus in the Gospel of St. John, "that they may be one, as we are one" (John 17:22) must have some institutional shape beyond our present situation. Needless to point out, while speculation has its place, no one quite knows what that institutional shape will be. Unless, however, Christians are prepared to

---

17. Wainwright, "Roman Catholic-Methodist Dialogue," 53. This essay has been reprinted with a "Postscript" in Wainwright, *Methodists in Dialogue*, 37–56.

18. Butler, *Methodists and Papists*, 203–4.

remain complacent about our fundamental lack of unity among ourselves, pledging and working for Christian unity must go on.

Too few Catholics and Methodists, including tragically too few systematic theologians on both parts, are really aware of ecumenical progress that has been made between the World Methodist Council and the Catholic Church. If indeed there is an ecumenical winter in our times, it is in no small part due to the failure of local Catholic clergy and Methodist ministers to be aware of this progress and to incorporate elements of it into their regular preaching and teaching. This letter written by John Wesley in 1749 might be one way of reminding us of the importance of Christian unity and pledging ourselves to work for it.

2

Bishop Lesslie Newbigin's *The Household of God*

The world will always consciously or unconsciously, judge what the church says by quantities. They will interpret the printed epistle by the living epistle.

LESSLIE NEWBIGIN.[1]

The Church of South India

Two respected Anglican ecumenical theologians of the last century, the brothers A. T. and R. P. C. Hanson, wrote these words in a book that they authored together on the church: "We are all guilty of dividing the church. Because we all of us together go to make up the being of the church in the world, none of us can escape responsibility for the state of internal schism in which we exist."[2] One might exaggerate the responsibility each of us has for the divided church of Christ, but one cannot evade the divided reality that is the church, and responsibility demands that we do all in our power individually and corporately to repair the damage to the church's unity

---

1. Newbigin, *Household of God*, 50.
2. Hanson, *Identity of the Church*, 45.

which our very separated existence represents. The Church of South India was a particular response in the mid-twentieth century to this situation.

The Church of South India came into being through a union of Anglican and Reformation churches in South India. Although controversial at its inception, especially for the Anglican Communion, today it has a membership of over five million, and is India's second largest Christian church after the Catholic Church. It came into existence just one month after India achieved independence from Britain in 1947. The inspiration for the Church of South India came from those words of our Blessed Lord in the Gospel of St. John 17:21: "That they all may be one, as you, Father, are in me and I am in you, that they also may be one in us, so that the world may believe that you have sent me." The Church of South India took as its motto those words of the prayer of Jesus, "That they all may be one," and became a milestone in the ecumenical world. This was the first time in history in which a union was effected between episcopal and non-episcopal churches. In this union four Christian traditions came together—Anglican (Episcopal), Congregational, Presbyterian, and Methodist. One of the most well-known and theologically articulate bishops of the Church of South India was Lesslie Newbigin.

Bishop Lesslie Newbigin (1909–98)

Bishop James Edward Lesslie Newbigin was a British theologian, missiologist, missionary, and author. Though originally ordained within the Church of Scotland (Presbyterian), Newbigin spent much of his career serving as a missionary in India and became affiliated with the Church of South India and the United Reformed Church, becoming one of the Church of South India's first bishops. He was an outstanding ecumenist, one whose life represents the ecumenical-church-in-mission in India and later in the United Kingdom, and one passionately supportive of the World Council of Churches.

Lesslie Newbigin was a prolific author who wrote on a wide range of theological topics, but he is best known for his contributions to missiology and ecclesiology. I was privileged to know Bishop Newbigin during the 1980s when we were both members of a theological discussion group in Birmingham (England), known as the "Open End." It was a very heterogeneous group that included such diverse theologians as John H. Hick (Presbyterian), Daniel W. Hardy and David F. Ford (Anglican), Frances M.

Young (Methodist), Michael D. Goulder (former Anglican), and the Anglican Bishop of Birmingham, Hugh Montefiore. In this diverse group Lesslie Newbigin brought to the table, as it were, not only a profound knowledge of theology and ecumenism, but a Christian commitment marked by a deep, personal piety. In his theological, intellectual, spiritual biography of Newbigin, Methodist theologian and veteran ecumenist Geoffrey Wainwright assesses the bishop's influential writing, preaching, teaching, and church guidance, concluding that his stature and range is comparable to the early Christian "Fathers of the Church."[3] A very high and well-deserved accolade indeed!

Five years after the inauguration of the Church of South India, during November 1952, Lesslie Newbigin gave the Kerr lectures in Trinity College, Glasgow, at that time the Faculty of Divinity of the University of Glasgow. These lectures were published eight years before Vatican II as *The Household of God*. If they were being published today, some sixty years later, by a Catholic bishop participating, for example, in the 2012 Synod of Bishops on the New Evangelization, they would be aptly entitled *Ecumenism and the New Evangelization*. The message is straightforward: evangelization must be accompanied, if it is to be persuasive, by a renewed commitment to ecumenism.[4]

The Household of God

Newbigin offers the following definition of the church from the beginning of this book: "The church itself is the visible company of those who have been called [by God] into the fellowship of his Son."[5] Towards the end of the book he calls the church "the sign, first-fruit and instrument of the Kingdom."[6] The church's visibility, the church's tangible witness to the kingdom of God is central in Christian ecclesiology. We may see an echo of Newbigin's thinking in the opening paragraph of Vatican II's Constitution on the Church: ". . . the church is in Christ a sacrament or instrumental sign of intimate union with God and of the unity of all humanity . . . ."[7] Signs

---

3. Wainwright, *Lesslie Newbigin*, v.

4. In his excellent *Introduction to Ecclesiology*, 151–52, Veli-Matti Kärkkäinen provides details of dissertations focusing on Newbigin's ecclesiology.

5. Newbigin, *Household of God*, 2.

6. Ibid., 146.

7. Tanner, ed., *Decrees*, vol. 2, 849.

are valuable for society when they are intelligible and easily legible. The question needs to be asked, "How legible is the church as a sign of the Kingdom of God?" The fact that so many Christians no longer walk with their churches may indicate among other things that the church's sign value is not particularly and obviously legible to them. Newbigin acknowledges this and recognizes the need for an ecclesiology that will speak to the modern condition. For Newbigin, the importance of ecclesiology today flows from three major factors: the breakdown of Christendom, the experience of the Christian mission, and the ecumenical movement.

The Breakdown of Christendom

What he describes as "the breakdown of Christendom" has to do with the rupture of the synthesis between the gospel and Western culture, "by which Christianity had become almost the folk-religion of Western Europe."[8] This synthesis between the gospel and Western culture began to spread and take root in the first millennium throughout Europe. While one might argue about how well defined and how deeply rooted Christendom was in that period, there can be no doubt that Christianity was woven into the tapestry of European life, both personally and at the institutional level. However, Newbigin sounds a caution: where Christendom is taken for granted, mission suffers. Once Christianity or Christendom had settled down, so to speak, the urgency of mission was no longer experienced. A certain entitled sense of complacency had settled in. Mission had to do with other places, not with Christianized Europe itself.

When the modern missionary movement from this European homeland of Christendom moved into other parts of the world, it brought the presuppositions of Christendom with it, but with one important qualification. The old Christendom had suffered the onslaught of the Enlightenment. Newbigin, in his brief historical overview of Christian history, tends to see the Enlightenment in rather negative terms. Where the church and culture had been at one before, now the church had to define distinctly and to defend itself more strenuously from the challenges of the wider culture. One result for him is clear—the fragmentation of societies and the atomization of the person. The traditional familial and social structures that upheld and sustained European society underwent a severe fragmentation. As society fragmented, so the individual person became isolated or atomized from

---

8. Newbigin, *Household of God*, 1.

the originating society of family, neighborhood, or region. Wherever this fragmentary and atomized Western society spread, "its characteristic product in Calcutta, Shanghai, or Johannesburg is the modern city into which myriads of human beings" are atomistically cast.[9] The sense of community that came into being with Christendom, where the whole population of Europe was identified more or less with the common culture of Christianity, became quickly eroded. The atomized self, increasingly cut off from a secure grounding in a tradition that offered a sense of stability and identity for the individual, was now adrift. If this was true when Newbigin was writing in 1952, it is much re-enforced today. All over the world, through the complex of forces described as "globalization," persons are severed—and sometimes also wish to sever themselves, often for political or economic reasons—from their originating and nurturing communities. A fundamental loneliness, or one might say alienation from both society and self, has become the experience of very many people. So, it is natural for people to ask if there is a family or a society to which they may belong and be truly at home, and if there is, where is it? Newbigin lays out a series of questions:

> If [there is a family of God on earth to which I can belong], where is it to be found, what are its marks and how is it related to, and distinguished from, the known communities of family, nation, and culture? What are its boundaries, its structure, its terms of membership? And how comes it that those who claim to be the spokesmen of that one holy fellowship are themselves at war with one another as to the fundamentals of its nature, and unable to agree to live together in unity and concord? The breakdown of Christendom has forced such questions as these to the front.[10]

In this series of questions examining the corporate conscience of the church, one notices especially the force of that last question, "How comes it that those who claim to be the spokesmen of that one holy fellowship are themselves at war with one another?" The lack of obvious and fruitful Christian unity is a counter-sign to the sign of the church, the sign that the church is of the kingdom of God.

---

9. Ibid., 3–4.
10. Ibid., 4.

The Experience of the Christian Mission

Too often the missionary movement was controlled by the old Christendom idea. The Christian "folk-religion of Europe" was taken throughout the world. In the course of the second millennium Christianity and Western culture, the old Christendom, were exported to Africa, Latin America, India, and the Orient. The church often functioned as Karl Rahner has it, as "an export firm which exported the European religion as a commodity it did not really want to change but sent throughout the world together with the rest of the culture and civilization it considered superior."[11] There was little attempt to establish an integral and organic relationship between the Christian gospel and the indigenous cultures in which it was being preached. The missionary movement took root, yes, in so many countries throughout the world. However, as many of these countries sought political independence from their former colonizers, they often sought also a form of the gospel more in accord with their own culture.

The Ecumenical Movement

> The ecumenical movement has been a byproduct of the missionary movement, arising out of the missionary experience of the church outside of the old Christendom, and enormously reinforced by the experience of churches within Christendom which have found themselves here also in a missionary situation face-to-face with new paganisms. It is important to bear this fact in mind, for the ecumenical movement will become fatally corrupted if it does not remain true to its missionary origins.[12]

The modern ecumenical movement was born during the 1910 Edinburgh Missionary Conference, with participants from all over what were then described as the missionary territories of the world. Now mission was to be everyone's business as a Christian. Newbigin recognizes that mission *within* the old European Christendom is now every bit as important as mission to the rest of the world was regarded then. This is the terrain of what Catholics have called the "new evangelization." The World Council of Churches, established in 1948 in Amsterdam, gave incipient institutional embodiment to the conviction that the church should be one, but it remains neutral

---

11. Rahner, "Theological Interpretation," 78.
12. Newbigin, *Household of God*, 10.

about the proper form and shape of that unity: "We are divided from one another, but Christ has made us his own, and he is not divided."[13]

The Three Embodiments of the Church

For Newbigin, there are three main embodiments of the church. As each is described, it may be felt that these embodiments are something of an ecclesiological caricature as things are seen today, but even if they are caricatures, there is enough realism in them to enable Newbigin's contrast to go ahead. Veli-Matti Kärkkäinen calls Newbigin's three embodiments "three ecclesiological streams."[14] This is in some ways preferable to Bishop Newbigin's nomenclature because it suggests or implies that streams flow into one another, something not so easy for embodiments. First, the embodiment of the church that emphasizes faith, that faith comes by hearing, and so, by the centrality of the preaching of the Word. This might be referred to as "classical Lutheranism," or more simply "Protestantism." It is the key emphasis of many of the Reformation communities, both in the sixteenth century and today. Second is the embodiment of the church that not only both honors preaching and acknowledges the necessity of faith, but is also centered on the sacramental activity of the church, rather than on the Word. This might be referred to as "classical Catholicism." The sacramental emphasis is central to Catholicism, both in its Western and in its Eastern forms. It might be framed in terms of Henri de Lubac's great axiom, "the Eucharist makes the church."[15] As a result of Vatican II, in the Constitutions on Revelation and on the Sacred Liturgy, Catholics are aware that there is not only no opposition between Word and Sacrament, but also that every celebration of sacrament is accompanied by a celebration of the Word. This awareness may not have been so obvious at the time Newbigin was writing in 1952. So, for the sake of his argument, we may say that the characteristic distinguishing mark of Catholicism is sacramental celebration. Third is the embodiment of the church that is more interested in the experienced effects of Christianity rather than in classical Protestantism or classical Catholicism. For want of a better term, Newbigin refers to this embodiment as "Pentecostalism."

---

13. Ibid., 13.
14. Kärkkäinen, *Introduction to Ecclesiology*, 154.
15. The term is used throughout de Lubac, *Corpus Mysticum*.

Newbigin criticizes the tendency in the Reformation traditions to downplay the importance of the historical and visible continuity of the church.

> It is necessary to seek penitently and realistically for the source of the tendency to endless fissiparation which has characterized Protestantism in its actual history. How has it come about that the vast majority of Protestant Christians are content to see the church of Jesus Christ split up into hundreds of separate sects, feel no sense of shame about such a situation, and sometimes even glory in it and claim the support of the New Testament for it?[16]

He lays great emphasis on the church as an actual divine humanity, as the real presence of God in human life and history. Furthermore, the church is God's invitation to humankind to enter into fellowship with himself. The church is constituted by the very presence of Christ.[17] Newbigin articulates what is perhaps most important about ecclesiology. The church is *there*. It can be seen, heard, and touched. It is visible. Using Newbigin's and Vatican II's language, the church is a "sign." It is not a kind of gnostic sect, essentially interior and intangible. This acknowledgment leads Newbigin to conclude: "The difficulty about what is purely spiritual is that it is apt to become purely private. We are not discarnate spirits and we enter into spiritual communion one with another only through our sense experience of sight, sound, and touch. Without this we quickly become prisoners of our own selfhood."[18]

It is most doubtful if the central Reformation ecclesial traditions, especially since the inception of the World Council of Churches and its many dialogues, would deny this visible embodiment of the church, at least in broad outline. "The Body of Christ in which Christians are members is a visible body, entrance into which is marked by the visible sign of baptism. In the same way the center of its ongoing life is a visible sign of bread broken together.... The visible center of this common life is the common sharing in the Lord's Supper, in which the members are made participants in his Body and Blood"[19] There may be different understandings of the sacraments, especially of the Eucharist, but classical Reformation traditions have not and do not wish to sever themselves from at least the celebration of baptism

---

16. Newbigin, *Household of God*, 53.
17. Ibid., 56-57.
18. Ibid., 58.
19. Ibid., 70-75.

and Eucharist. In many ways, the sacrament of baptism is less problematic than the sacrament of the Eucharist. More is agreed about baptism than about Eucharist. Where agreement about the latter is lacking, and Christian communities continue Sunday after Sunday to celebrate their own exclusivist Eucharists, then the fundamental unity of the church is diminished. The Methodist theologian and veteran ecumenist, Geoffrey Wainwright, who is also the accomplished biographer of Bishop Newbigin, points this out very clearly: "Each community may know reconciliation with God, but as long as the communities are not reconciled with one another, they can hardly bear convincing witness before the world to Christ's reconciling work; for if the horizontal corollary is not in evidence, even the vertical achievement may be called into question."[20] For Wainwright, and indeed for traditional eucharistic theology, the Eucharist is not only a sign of the church's unity but also brings about or effects that unity. Where separate eucharistic tables are the norm, the unity of the church is impaired.

This is an issue that has been taken with great seriousness by leaders in the ecumenical movement. Some thirty years after the publication of Bishop Newbigin's *The Household of God*, the World Council of Churches published in 1982 a milestone document entitled *Baptism, Eucharist and Ministry*, in which the council invited its members to recognize within the parameters of this text their own particular understanding of baptism, Eucharist, and ministry.[21] Generally speaking, the member churches of the World Council of Churches had a strong positive response to this document, although differences still exist.[22] These differences are still being worked on by ecumenical theologians and their communities throughout the Christian world. One thinks of, for example, the outstanding work of the Presbyterian theologian George Hunsinger, the subject of chapter 8 in this book. When Newbigin wrote in 1952 that "the visible center of this common life is the common sharing in the Lord's Supper, in which the members are made participants in his Body and Blood," he was setting the agenda for ecumenical reflection and action over the next decades.

Newbigin recognizes that even in Reformation traditions that are very critical of traditional Catholic ecclesiology, they all accept in practice "a certain authority over the preaching of the word and the administration of

---

20. Wainwright, *Ecumenical Moment*, 61.

21. World Council of Churches, *Baptism, Eucharist and Ministry*, This document is often referred to as the "Lima Text" since it was promulgated in Lima, Peru.

22. See Wainwright, *Reformation Over?* 30.

the sacraments."[23] So, using the classical, traditional terminology there is always some sense of "apostolic succession." This notion has always been very important to Catholic Christians—the Orthodox, Roman Catholics, and Anglicans. Newbigin points out that in perhaps different ways this theological principle of apostolic succession is important also for the churches of the Reformation. He writes:

> The same Luther who denied in principle that the church could exclude him from the communion of Christ, in later life placed the use of the power of the keys among the essential marks of the church alongside of the word and sacraments. The followers of Calvin and Knox, who had both absolutely denied that ministerial succession is a mark of the true church, are found asserting a perpetual succession of presbyters. And the followers of John Wesley, who had performed an act of ordination for which he had no ecclesiastical authority, would probably be more horrified than any other body of Christians if one of their members today did the same. . . . [These things] are a deeply impressive testimony to the fact that it belongs to the nature of the church to have a visible and continuing structure.[24]

Having made this emphasis abundantly clear, Newbigin equally emphasizes what might be called the importance of "anonymous apostolic succession":

> No one who is not spiritually blind or worse can fail to acknowledge that God has signally and abundantly blessed the preaching, sacraments, and ministry of great bodies which can claim no uninterrupted ministerial succession from the apostles, but who have contributed at least as much as those who have remained within it to the preaching of the Gospel, the conversion of sinners, and the building up of the saints in holiness.[25]

If the marks of holiness are to be seen in the lives of Christians in the Reformation traditions, then somehow, perhaps in ways that are not easily articulated by Roman Catholics or the Orthodox, there are present elements of apostolic succession, albeit perhaps "anonymously."

When it comes to Pentecostalism, the . . .

---

23. Newbigin, *Household of God*, 59.
24. Ibid., 77.
25. Ibid., 84.

central element is the conviction that the Christian life is a matter of the experienced power and presence of the Holy Spirit today; that neither orthodoxy of doctrine nor impeccability of succession can take the place of this; that an excessive emphasis upon those immutable elements in the Gospel upon which Orthodox Catholicism and Protestantism have concentrated attention may, and in fact often does, result in a church which is a mere shell, having the form of a church but not the life; that if we would answer the question "Where is the church?," we must ask "Where is the Holy Spirit recognizably present with power?"[26]

Note the importance of the adverb "recognizably." If the Holy Spirit is present, then for the Pentecostalist that presence should be verifiable. It should make a difference, and this difference coincides with the experience of the earliest Christians as expressed in the New Testament. This is how Newbigin puts it: "The Holy Spirit may be the last article of the Creed but in the New Testament it is the first fact of experience."[27] Experiencing the Holy Spirit is more important than doctrine about the Holy Spirit. Now, obviously, there cannot be experience without some kind of doctrine, however implicit or latent. But, if we bear with Newbigin's ecclesiological portraits, the point is that this characteristic of the Pentecostal ecclesial experience must be taken seriously. Indeed, one may appropriately see it present in different degrees throughout the entire history of the church, beginning with the Corinthians in the New Testament, the Montanists of the second century, and so on to the enthusiasts of every Christian generation, as they emphasize the centrality of experience over doctrine. So, the Catholic-Protestant debate needs to be three-cornered, to include the Pentecostal forms of Christianity.

Newbigin acknowledges a certain reluctance on the part of more traditional or classical ecclesiologies to engage Pentecostalism:

> We are uncomfortable without definite principles by which we may guide our steps. We fear uncharted country and the fanatics of all kinds who, upon the alleged authority of the Holy Spirit, summon us with strident cries in all directions simultaneously. Only those who have never borne the heavy burden of pastoral responsibility will mock at the cautious spirit of the ecclesiastic. But on the other hand let us admit that according to the New Testament we are summoned precisely to the task of "discerning the

26. Ibid., 95.
27. Ibid., 96.

spirits"; that it is there taken for granted both that the Holy Spirit is free and sovereign, able to work in ways that demand rethinking of our traditional categories, and that he himself gives to the church the necessary gifts by which he may be known (e.g., 1 Corinthians 12:10).[28]

Having said this, there must be balance. Newbigin continues:

> When the claim to possession by the Spirit, attested perhaps by abnormal signs of spiritual power, is made the ground for treating the unity and order of the church with contempt, and for despising the great mass of "nominal Christians" in whom only the virtues which we have come to regard as normal for a Christian are to be seen, we must say bluntly as St. Paul did, that this is not the work of the Spirit but of the flesh. There is one Body as there is one Spirit, and there are no grounds for thinking that we can try to separate one from the other without disastrous error.[29]

Traditional, more established Christian traditions have tended to ignore Pentecostals, and so Pentecostals have tended to ignore more established and traditional ways of doing theology. Newbigin as a "father of the church" recognizes the theological absurdity of this mutual ignorance. Since *The Household of God* considerable headway has been made with Pentecostals, but it is not unfair to say that there exists a degree of mutual discomfort here. If church unity is to be taken seriously, if there is one Body as there is one Spirit, all Christians must emerge from their comfort zones genuinely to encounter, engage, and enter into deep conversation about their mutual love for the Lord Jesus, and so for the unity of the church as the sacrament or sign of his presence in the world.

Newbigin's approach to ecclesiology is never exclusivist. In developing his classical Protestant, classical Catholic, and Pentecostal approaches to the meaning of the church, his constant intention is to be all-embracing. Not only to be all-embracing in principle as it were, but to be all-embracing in practice. In practical terms, Newbigin identifies with what is now called receptive ecumenism, that is, to learn all that it is possible to learn from other Christian traditions without expecting, in a sense, anything in return. That is certainly implied in the theology and ecclesiology of Lesslie Newbigin. Without—in my judgment unfortunately—making any explicit reference to the contribution of Bishop Newbigin, one contemporary ecumenical

---

28. Ibid., 106.
29. Ibid., 116.

theologian understands what Newbigin is about: "For this process of overcoming stasis to begin, it requires some to take responsibility, to take the initiative, and this regardless of whether others are ready to reciprocate. As the therapeutic adage goes, 'We cannot change others. We can only change ourselves and, thereby, the way we relate to others.'"[30] This is what Newbigin's *The Household of God* is all about, and what he exemplified in person throughout his life.

Mission, or the New Evangelization

Newbigin quotes the mid-twentieth-century Protestant theologian Emil Brunner as saying "The church exists by mission as fire exists by burning," and he himself adds that: "[The church] has its being, so to say, in the magnetic field between Christ and the world. Its *koinonia* in him is a participation in his apostolate to the world."[31] This is exactly the point of view that comes to expression, albeit in different ways, in Vatican II's decree *On the Missionary Activity of the Church* and the *Pastoral Constitution on the Church in the Modern World*. This is an older phrasing of what many contemporaries refer to as the "new evangelization." The church exists to be missionary; the church is mission, just as the whole event of Jesus Christ, the whole event of the incarnation is mission.

"It is no accident that the modern movement for Christian reunion is a by-product of the modern missionary movement, and that its chief impetus has come from the areas where the church has been formed by missionary expansion outside the frontiers of the old Christendom."[32] The reference is to the Edinburgh Missionary Conference of 1910. Missionaries from all over the world spearheaded the modern ecumenical movement. Thus, disunity among Christians for Newbigin destroys mission. Hence the abiding importance of ecumenism, especially of this three-cornered ecumenism: Catholic (including, of course, the Orthodox and the Anglicans), Protestant, and Pentecostal. Newbigin writes:

> I do not think that a resolute dealing with our divisions will come except in the context of a quite new acceptance on the part of all the churches of the obligation to bring the Gospel to every creature; nor do I think that the world will believe that Gospel until it sees

30. Murray, "Receptive Ecumenism," 15.
31. Ibid., 162–63.
32. Ibid., 173.

more evidence of its power to make us one. These two tasks—mission and unity—must be prosecuted together and in indissoluble relation one with another.[33]

In our contemporary terms, Newbigin is reaffirming that the new evangelization will not work and cannot last unless it is also fueled by a passion for mission that is undergirded by an equal passion for Christian unity.

Towards the end of his book Newbigin writes:

> I began these lectures by asking: "What is the manner of our incorporation in Christ?" I have tried to show that all the three answers which we looked at are true; we are made members in him by hearing and believing the gospel (classical Protestantism), by being received sacramentally into the visible fellowship of his people (classical Catholicism), and both of these only through the living presence of the Holy Spirit (Pentecostalism). At the same time I tried to show that when any one of them was taken as alone decisive, error and distortion followed.[34]

Protestant Christians, Catholic Christians, and Pentecostal Christians in his view need not only to recognize these three ecclesial categorizations, even if they are to be understood in part as caricatures, but they also need to integrate those life-giving aspects of the gospel found in the other into their own living of the good news.[35]

Conclusion

Bishop Lesslie Newbigin devoted the last twenty-five years of his life to a project that he called "The Gospel and Our Culture." Recognizing that Europe, the old Christendom having completely collapsed, is now itself a mission field, Newbigin describes the situation in these terms:

> The long syncretistic relation between Christianity and Western culture has now developed into a situation where the specificity of the gospel is almost lost, absorbed into the relativism, individualism and narcissism of Western culture. It is now necessary for preachers in the Western world to recognize that they are in a missionary situation where the Bible is no longer authoritative Scripture, and the name of Jesus, freely used in swearing, does not

33. Ibid., 174.
34. Ibid., 148.
35. See Wainwright, *Embracing Purpose*, 66.

> refer to any well-known person.... The task is to recover the full meaning of the words we use in Christian discourse, and that can only happen when the Bible, in its canonical wholeness, recovers its place as Scripture.[36]

Recovering the place of the Bible as Scripture is a challenge equally for what Newbigin called classical Protestantism and classical Catholicism. It is increasingly a sad fact that Protestants and Catholics no longer have a deep appreciation of the Scriptures. Perhaps what Newbigin called the third way of Pentecostalism can help here. Pentecostals' spiritual quest

> has led them to spend more time reading their Bibles, more time in prayer, more time with like-minded seekers ... who believed ... that "Jesus Christ is the same, yesterday, today, and forever" (Hebrews 13:8). If Jesus Christ was truly the same in our day as he had been in Bible days they reasoned, then surely his promises were as true today as they had been when he walked the land of Israel.[37]

I cannot believe that it is impossible for the mainline churches to learn this lesson from their Pentecostal brothers and sisters. The expanded lectionaries that are now part of the Sunday worship experience for most Christians in our country would be an excellent place to rediscover the importance of the Bible as Scripture. Small Bible groups, led by adequately informed leaders, in inter-confessional situations could be a wonderful way of trying to re-establish the centrality of Scripture for Christian living and witness. In other words, we would be learning from the Pentecostals.

Although it is many years since I first encountered and read Lesslie Newbigin's *The Household of God*, the recent Synod of Bishops in Rome (2012), discussing all aspects of the "new evangelization," reminded me of his powerful message. Many of the Synod fathers are re-emphasizing the importance of ecumenism. Bishop Newbigin's little book may be of considerable help in this regard, and his passion for the unity of the church may ignite a similar passion among ourselves.

---

36. Newbigin, "Missions," 336.
37. Robeck, "Holy Spirit and Unity," 365.

3

Vatican II, Decree on Ecumenism

Nobody doubts any longer that something happened at Vatican II, but what happened is not so obvious.

MASSIMO FAGGIOLI.[1]

In a few years' time, the Council will be nobody's living memory.

NICHOLAS LASH.[2]

Pope John XXIII and His Council

Once upon a time, at the beginning of the twentieth century, there was a young priest whose name was Angelo from a small diocese in the north of Italy. When Angelo was born in 1881, John Henry Newman was still alive in England and would remain so for almost the first decade of Angelo's life. "Newman was a prophet with a mission to the Church in the modern age; he was one of the first to perceive history as a process of development and

---

1. Faggioli, *Vatican II*, 112.
2. Lash, *Theology for Pilgrims*, 227.

apply this to Christianity."³ It is unclear if Angelo had ever read anything by Newman, but he certainly shared his prophetic perspective.

Angelo showed some scholarly promise, and so in 1901 he went on to complete his studies in Rome. Among his fellow students in Rome was Ernesto Buonaiuti (1881–1946). Buonaiuti was probably the most prominent Italian condemned and excommunicated for Modernism. Since personal friendships were discouraged in the seminary, students going out for a walk were assigned a companion, and so Angelo and Buonaiuti often walked together around Rome. Buonaiuti was ordained one year before Angelo, and in fact assisted at the latter's ordination. A brilliant young scholar, Buonaiuti was dismissed from his teaching post in 1915 for holding Modernist views, and eventually in 1926 he was excommunicated.

Among Angelo's professors at the seminary was the church historian Msgr. Umberto Benigni, who was to become the mastermind behind the anti-Modernist spy campaign under Pope Pius X. "He contributed to Angelo's choice of history as his special field."⁴ Another of his professors was Eugenio Pacelli, the future Pope Pius XII, who taught canon law. Angelo loved his studies. In 1903 the young seminarian was to write in his journal: "Tomorrow the lectures begin again: I feel a need and a passionate desire to study.... I feel a restless longing to know everything, to study all the great authors, to familiarize myself with the scientific movement in all it manifestations."⁵ This is experientially what may be described as an unrestricted desire to understand. This unrestricted desire won for the young seminarian a prize for Hebrew. His passion for study shows him breaking out of the narrow confines of the traditional seminary curriculum of the time, dominated by neo-scholastic manuals of philosophy and theology, and moving into a richer and broader way of thinking, a way of thinking in which historical context and development has pride of place. Angelo was ordained to the priesthood in 1904, and was appointed secretary to his bishop. At the same time at the local seminary he taught apologetics, church history, and patristics. New ways of studying church history were emerging on the scene, typified by the work of the great Monsignor Louis Duchesne.⁶ Angelo was using Duchesne's *History of the Early Church* to

---

3. Trevor, *Pope John*, 84.

4. Hebblethwaite, *John XXIII*, 18.

5. Pope John XXIII, *Journal of a Soul*, 110–11.

6. See the admirable account of Louis Duchesne in Frend, *From Dogma to History*, 100–143.

prepare for his lectures. Historical consciousness was making its impact felt in the field of theology, and this appealed to the young priest-professor. Nevertheless, his use of Duchesne made him suspect in the new anti-Modernist regime. Duchesne's three-volume history of the early church was to be placed on the *Index of Forbidden Books* in 1912. Undoubtedly because of his interest in church history, and the liberating perspectives that follow from such study, Angelo was unjustly accused of Modernism. Angelo loved the church. He would never have taught against the church, nor would he ever do anything to harm the church. But to be suspected of Modernism was too much. And so in June 1908, Angelo spent several days with Bishop Geremia Bonomelli of Cremona. The bishop was well known for the generosity of his views, and two years after meeting with Angelo Roncalli he sent a letter of best wishes for the success of the World Missionary Conference in Edinburgh in 1910. Here was a Catholic bishop well ahead of his time, and for this young priest, a kindred soul. The year 1908, in fact, was also the year in which Bishop Bonomelli wrote: "Perhaps a great ecumenical council, which would discuss rapidly, freely and publicly the great problems of religious life, would draw the attention of the world to the church, stimulate faith, and open up new ways for the future."[7] Angelo returned to his diocese encouraged and with great hope in his heart for the future of the church.

In 1958, Angelo became Pope John XXIII. One of the first things he did as Pope was he asked to see his file at the Holy Office. The file had been marked "Suspected of Modernism." As part of the evidence he found in the file a postcard that had been addressed to him by his friend Ernesto Buonaiuti. Pope John XXIII wrote on the file: "I was never a Modernist." He was preeminently a churchman, never undermining the church's mission or message, but he was far from closed to the exciting and new ideas that were in the air. Three months after his election on January 25, 1959, at the celebration of Vespers for the conclusion of the week of prayer for Christian unity, he announced what were to be three projects of his pontificate:

1. The convocation of a diocesan synod for the diocese of Rome.
2. The reform of the Code of Canon Law.
3. The calling of a new ecumenical council.

Almost exactly fifty years after his visit with Bishop Bonomelli Angelo Roncalli took up Bonomelli's idea of a great ecumenical council. This third project surprised everyone. "No bishop alive in 1959 had any personal

---

7. Cited in Hebblethwaite, *John XXIII*, 33.

recollection of an ecumenical Council; councils were simply not part of the consciousness of the church."[8] This was to be a pastoral council to open up the church, not to barricade it in. For John there were to be no condemnations or excommunications. The proposal met with resistance from the Roman Curia. To be fair, Pope John had no detailed blueprint for what he wanted the council to achieve. Nonetheless, as Eamon Duffy writes: "The Council he had called, with no very clear notion of what it might do, proved to be the most revolutionary Christian event since the Reformation."[9]

The special quality of the Pope's opening address to the council was optimism. This contrasts with a certain negativism or even pessimism toward the world since the time of Pope Pius IX (pope from 1846–78). Some would say much further, for example, church historian Edward Hales: "The general temper of the church, since the seventeenth century, has inclined toward pessimism. She has evidently been more concerned to raise the barriers, to stave off further losses, than to risk collaborating with others . . . ."[10] Doom and gloom were not the Johannine style, as John himself stated: "It seems to us necessary to express our complete disagreement with these prophets of doom, who give news only of catastrophes, as though the world were nearing its end."[11]

What Happened at Vatican II?

Any good church historian will point out that Vatican II was decades in the making, gradually and slowly but decidedly, perhaps especially with the kind of theological thinking associated with the *nouvelle théologie* that emerged in France and Germany during the 1930s and 40s. However, the point has been exceptionally well made by historian Stephen Schloesser that in the post-1945 world the Second Vatican Council was a necessary response to momentous shifts in history and culture in the mid-twentieth century. He points to shifts such as World War II, the Holocaust, the Cold War between the USSR and its empire and the West, the atomic bomb exemplified at Hiroshima and Nagasaki, and the slow but ongoing process of decolonization with the consequent ending of Western hegemony, heralded

---

8. Gaillardetz and Clifford, *Keys to the Council*, xii.
9. Duffy, *Saints and Sinners*, 360.
10. Hales, *Pope John and His Revolution*, 138–39.
11. Ibid., 139.

by the independence of India from Britain in 1947. These shifts pushed the church to think about its own identity in this very fast-changing world.

In this world marked by the increasing fragmentation of humankind as a result of these shifts, the fragmentation already noted in Lesslie Newbigin's *The Household of God*, Vatican II emphasized the unity of humankind, a unity found sacramentalized in the church. By the time the council had ended in December 1965, maintains Schloesser, a broad and expanded ecclesial horizon had emerged: "While not neglecting the details of the church's internal life, it had stepped back from perspectives specific to Catholicism, Christianity, and even religion in general. It had stepped back to see the world—humanity, history, existence—from the perspective of the broadest possible horizons. It asked anew what its purpose was—and what the purpose of Christian believers was—in a world populated by nations and cultures whose difference and diversity were finally being acknowledged in a postcolonialist world."[12]

This was a church emerging and indeed, was forced to emerge from the parameters of the anti-modern, fortress-like mentality that had characterized it in the nineteenth century and into the mid-twentieth century. If world-changing events had made the council virtually a moral necessity, its closest parallel in the conciliar tradition would probably be the Fourth Lateran Council in 1215. This was the greatest reforming council of the Middle Ages, opening up both theological and ecclesial reforms. If Vatican II was the climax of theological development and ecclesial reform over a period of one hundred years, it was so in a pastoral way, as already noted. That is to say, it was not specifically concerned with a particular threat or a particular challenge, unless one wants to say that a certain opening up to the modern world constituted the challenge. That seems to have been at least implicit in the two aims that Pope John XXIII had for the council when he announced it on January 25, 1959: first, "the enlightenment, edification, and joy of the entire Christian people"; and second, "a renewed cordial invitation to the faithful of the separated churches to participate with us in this feast of grace and brotherhood." Many point out that these aims are not especially clear and specific. While that is true, it seems to me that they indicate a "certain opening up" to the modern world. The aims are positively expressed, and

12. Stephen Schloesser, SJ, "Against Forgetting," 138. Schloesser is, of course, not the only scholar to make this important point. For example, the church historian Giuseppe Alberigo indicates, suggest, and hints as much in his *Brief History of Vatican II*, but, as the very title points out, Alberigo's treatment is "brief," that is to say, contextually underdeveloped.

the second aim was not an invitation to return to Rome but rather to participate in a global movement of Christian renewal.[13]

The directing principle of Vatican II was provided by Pope John XXIII in two buzzwords: the Italian term *aggiornamento*, a word that means something like "bringing up to date" or "modernizing" and the French term *ressourcement*, a return to the sources. In reality, *ressourcement* was the primary engine of *aggiornamento*. "*Ressourcement* is not an alternative to *aggiornamento*, but the means of its achievement."[14] The 2,540 voting council fathers met in St. Peter's Basilica itself, remodeled for this purpose into an auditorium. The council consisted of four chronologically distinct meetings: the first session, from October 11 to December 8, 1962; the second session, from September 29 to December 4, 1963; the third session from September 14 to November 21, 1964; the fourth and final session, from September 14 to December 8 1965.

Seventy draft preparatory documents were drawn up by curial commissions, but without any particular plan for their deliberation. The situation was a recipe for conciliar disaster. This led the Belgian Cardinal Suenens to speak to Pope John in March 1962. This is Suenens's recollection of the event: Suenens to Pope John: "'Who is working on an overall plan for the Council?' 'Nobody,' said Pope John. Suenens: 'But there will be total chaos. How do you imagine we can discuss seventy-two schemata . . . ?' 'Yes,' John agreed, 'We need a plan. . . . Would you like to do one?'"[15] With consultation and collaboration with other European cardinals Suenens drew up a plan for the council which was sent to Rome, but did not go anywhere. In September 1962, Cardinal Frings of Cologne had a memorandum sent to Rome and drawn up by the theologian he was taking to the council to the effect that the language of the texts to be debated and ultimately promulgated should not be the scholastic and manualist language of the traditional Roman textbooks, but rather "the vital language of Scripture and the Church Fathers." Frings's theologian who drafted this memorandum was the young Joseph Ratzinger.[16] Many, including Joseph Ratzinger, were utterly dissatisfied with the scholastic register of discourse in which the draft documents had been written.

---

13. Cited in O'Malley, "Introduction," 3.
14. Lash, *Theology for Pilgrims*, 231.
15. Suenens, "A Plan for the Whole Council," 88–91.
16. See Wicks, "Six Texts," 233–311.

During the very first week of the council, October 1962, two things happened that were to change the course of events. First, the assembled bishops made the decision to elect from among themselves who would be appointed to the various commissions, effectively displacing the curial control of the council. Second, Cardinal Montini, later to become Pope Paul VI, wanted to know whether there was any plan for the deliberation of the council documents. With the approval of Pope John, Montini edited Suenens's plan already submitted, and so the council got underway.

Almost immediately the Second Vatican Council was polarized. How to describe the polarization is a difficult challenge. Since at least the time of the French Revolution in 1789, the terms *conservative* and *liberal* have entered our common vocabulary, and perhaps we are simply stuck with them, even in the church. At the same time, Christians must recognize that whether self-styled conservative or liberal or for that matter anything else, each and everyone remains a baptized member of Christ's holy body. With that in mind, let us look at how the various documents from the council were produced. The various draft documents that had been produced by the Roman Curia were rejected by a majority of the bishops. They were after something quite different, an ecclesial perspective that was more open and sensitive to the actual pastoral realities they faced in their dioceses throughout the world. At the same time, many of them were trapped—if that is not too strong a word—in the neo-scholasticism of their own seminary days, without too much awareness of developments in the study of the Bible and of the move from classical to historical consciousness.[17] In a very real sense, the Catholic bishops of the world were going back to school! Apart altogether from being in St. Peter's Basilica for episcopal debate and discussion, many of the bishops spent time in the evening attending lectures by various theologians who were at the council in the capacity of "experts" or *periti*. One fine example of a bishop back at school is provided by Bishop Albino Luciani, later to become Pope John Paul I. He made the effort to spend the afternoons studying in his room. Luciani wrote of his experience: "Everything I learned at the Gregorian [University] is useless now. I have to become a student again. Fortunately I have an African bishop as a neighbor in the bleachers in the Council Hall, who gives me the texts of the experts of the German bishops. That way I can better prepare myself."[18]

---

17. Fagan, "Theology in the Making," 69. Fagan is echoing language made possible by Bernard J. F. Lonergan, SJ.

18. Cited in Gaillardetz, "What Can We Learn?" 91–92.

Vatican II, Decree on Ecumenism

It was inevitable from an historical perspective that the polarization would continue. Conservatives—for want of a better word—felt that Pope John XXIII had introduced liberal reforms in the church that led to clamors for even greater change. Liberals—for want of a better word—felt that the changes were a good beginning, but there was a need to press much further ahead. While describing the pre-history of *Lumen Gentium* (The Constitution on the Church) Cardinal Suenens provides an accurate glimpse of the two different and fundamental approaches to theological reflection at the council:

> There was here a confrontation between two different conceptions of the church. The Holy Office had prepared a draft text inscribed by an ecclesiology that was deeply marked by the canonical and institutional aspects of the church, rather than emphasizing and giving priority to the spiritual and evangelistic aspects. In our eyes, it was a matter of stepping out of a legalistic ecclesiology and into an ecclesiology of communion, centered on the mystery of the church in its most profound Trinitarian dimensions.[19]

By the end of the fourth and final session in 1965, Vatican II would promulgate sixteen documents: four constitutions, nine decrees, and three declarations. "No document was opposed in the final vote by more than a handful of bishops. But there was a price to be paid for this high level of unanimity. Significant compromises were made. While achieving full consensus was unlikely, the support of opposing sides of an issue was often secured by juxtaposing, sometimes in the same paragraph, alternative formulations." Compromise and juxtaposition, however, made it possible "for various ideological camps to appeal to certain passages that appeared to support their particular ecclesiastical agenda while excluding other texts."[20] That is simply the way we human beings are. We do not immediately agree about things, even central and important things, in a uniform fashion, nor should we expect to. If we recognize anything about ourselves authentically, it is that the truth, any important truth that informs our lives, is never just out there now to be picked up and reiterated, but rather human beings agonize towards truth and to its performance. Nicholas Lash writes with great accuracy: "A church in which there were no serious disagreements would be dead. Disagreement about things that matter deeply to the disputants may create tensions but does not, of itself, do damage to the bonds

---

19. Suenens, *Memories and Hopes*, 132.
20. Gaillardetz and Clifford, *Keys to the Council*, xv–xvi.

of charity or threaten sacramental unity."[21] That is how we should be acting as Christians. We do not have to be clones of one another. We do not have to think exactly like one another in a uniform fashion. We do not have to excommunicate those with whom we find ourselves in some measure of disagreement. "We can resist the compulsion to evict those who disagree with us."[22] But we do need to be bonded in charity so that the world may believe.

The Decree on Ecumenism

The Decree on Ecumenism is in point of fact a very short document of some thirteen pages or so. Although it is now a half century old, it re-pays careful reading. This is especially the case when one recognizes that ecumenism was far from being a top priority of the Catholic Church in the twentieth century prior to the council. Veteran Catholic ecumenical theologian George Tavard maintains that Pope Pius XI's encyclical letter on ecumenism *Mortalium Animos* of 1928 is not as negative as it is often taken to be. He believes that it gave something of a necessary warning to Roman Catholics not to dilute the richness of their received faith and tradition.[23] Fair enough. And although it is something of a caricature, nonetheless Eamon Duffy's description of the same encyclical responding to the growing ecumenical movement captures the at-large Catholic attitude to ecumenism: "[Pope Pius XI's] least attractive encyclical. . . . He rubbished the infant ecumenical movement. . . . The encyclical made it clear that the ecumenical message of the Vatican for the other churches was simple and uncompromising: 'Come in slowly with your hands above your head.'"[24] Pius condemned what he called the "pan-Christians" of the ecumenical movement. He assumed the movement to be a lowest common denominator form of Christianity. His reaction to ecumenism with the Reformation traditions was not particularly different from that of his predecessor, Pope Benedict XV. It was largely a "return to Rome" approach. Pius forbade for all practical purposes any formal conversations or dialogues with Reformation Christians.[25] A more

21. Lash, *Theology for Pilgrims*, 231.
22. Radcliffe, *What Is the Point?* 212.
23. Tavard, *Two Centuries of Ecumenism*, 98.
24. Duffy, *Saints and Sinners*, 346.
25. Pope Pius XI's attitude to Orthodox/Eastern Christians was different. See the brief account in Cummings, *History of the Popes*, 60.

Vatican II, Decree on Ecumenism

positive response to the ecumenical movement came about with Pope Pius XII, albeit a limited positive response. Against this background, Vatican II's Decree on Ecumenism is a breath of fresh air. "By its cogent reasoning it carried the Catholic Church out of its previous isolation and plunged it into the mainstream of the ecumenical movement."[26]

"The restoration of unity among all Christians is one of the principal concerns of the second Vatican Synod."[27] This is the very first sentence of the decree and that spells out the vision with great clarity: restoring Christian unity is a principal concern of Vatican II. The same first paragraph acknowledges success of the ecumenical movement and acknowledges the Catholic desire to be associated with this movement in the restoration of Christian unity.

Chapter 1 of the decree is entitled "Catholic Principles of Ecumenism." After noting the words of the Lord in St. John's Gospel—"that they may all be one, even as you, Father, are in me, and I in you, that they also may be one in us; so that the world may believe that you have sent me" (John 17:21)—the passage goes on to insist on the centrality of the Eucharist in this enterprise of Christian unity. "In his church [Christ] instituted the wonderful sacrament of the Eucharist by which the unity of the church is both signified and made a reality" (paragraph 2). This sentence and the vision behind the sentence express the conviction that at the heart of Christian unity lays the Eucharist, whose purpose is to show forth, to signify, and to effect the unity of the church. It does not seem merely coincidental that this conviction should occur at this point in the document. If the liturgy and especially the Eucharist, as taught by Vatican II's Constitution on the Sacred Liturgy, is the center, source, and origin of the church's life, then it must also be this with regard to ecumenism. The paragraph goes on to insist on the traditional principles of Catholic ecclesiology that one would expect—one body, one Spirit, one baptism, the episcopate, and the Petrine ministry. From a historical point of view, the text acknowledges that the schismatic tendency has been in the Christian church from the very beginning: 1 Corinthians 11:18–19; Galatians 1:6–9; 1 John 2:18–19. In subsequent centuries, however, this schismatic tendency became even stronger so that large communities became separated from the full communion of the Catholic Church, but, the decree insists, "people of both sides were to

---

26. Dulles, "Decree on Ecumenism," 17.

27. Tanner, SJ, ed., *Decrees*, vol. 2, 908. An excellent but brief resume and discussion of the decree may be found in Gaillardetz and Clifford, *Keys to the Council*, 148–59.

blame" (paragraph 3). Historians have always known that ecclesial schism was never intelligible in terms of one side or one cause only. History is much messier and more complex than that. That is why it is good to find the express acknowledgment in the document that blame for schism lay with both sides, that is to say with Catholics, as well as with those being separated from Catholicism. Too often popular historical representations insisted that blame rested solely with those who separated themselves from Rome. Catholics are to look upon other Christians as their separated sisters and brothers, with respect and love, and to accept as fundamental that baptism places Christians in other traditions "in some kind of communion with the Catholic Church, even though this communion is imperfect" (paragraph 3). This is very important because the insistence is that unity already exists through baptism, and the ecumenical cause is to take that unity of partial communion into full communion. In line with this acknowledgment there is the recognition that in those communities separated from the Catholic Church there exist gifts from the Spirit that help to build up holiness of life in the church. These gifts include "the written word of God; the life of grace; faith, hope and charity, with the other interior gifts of the Holy Spirit, and visible elements too" (paragraph 3). The text quickly goes on to assert that differences exist in varying degrees between other Christian communities and the Catholic Church, but it builds from what is held in common first. Jean Tillard confirms and strengthens this perspective when he writes: "It is now time for the confessional churches to discern, confirm, consolidate and defend this God-given reality by which they are united, that is the presence of the one Church of God (as such) in each of them, whatever may be the mode of this presence."[28]

The insistence on the promotion of Christian unity is to be a concern not only of church leaders and clergy, but of "all the Catholic faithful" (paragraph 4). Then follows some practical instructions for how to work on this project of Christian unity, instructions that in part echo John Wesley's *Letter to a Roman Catholic*: To be avoided,

> First, every effort to avoid expressions, judgments and actions which do not represent the condition of our separated sisters and brothers with truth and fairness and so make mutual relations with them more difficult; then, "dialogue" between competent experts at meetings of Christians from different churches and communities. . . . Finally, all are led to examine their own faithfulness

---

28. Tillard, "*Ex Tenebris Lux*," 201.

to Christ's will for the church and accordingly to undertake with vigor the task of renewal and reform (paragraph 4).

In this fashion, when all obstacles have been overcome, "all Christians will at last, in a common celebration of the Eucharist, be gathered into the unity of the one and only church" and this unity "subsists" in the Catholic Church (paragraph 4). Yet again, we see in the text that the Eucharist is the central point of Christian unity. And we see also, and by implication, that the unity of Christ's church "subsists" in the Catholic Church so that elements of this unity of Christ's church may be found in other ecclesial traditions. The language is to some extent cumbersome, but compared with the polemics of the last half millennium the language is generous. Elements of what we might call "churchness" may be found outside the boundaries of the Roman Catholic Church.[29]

Chapter 2 of the decree is entitled "The Practice of Ecumnism." This chapter begins by reiterating what has already been said that the restoration of unity is the concern of all the baptized, and not simply of a few. Catholics are encouraged when it is appropriate and circumstances permit to pray with other Christians. "Yet worship in common is not to be considered as a means to be used indiscriminately for the restoration of Christian unity" (paragraph 8). This particular phrase "worship in common," in Latin *communicatio in sacris*, is a technical term for eucharistic sharing or intercommunion. At the same time, the council fathers insist that while "witness to the unity of the church generally forbids common worship, the grace to be had from it sometimes commends this practice" (paragraph 8). In other words, there is no absolute veto in respect of eucharistic sharing, and the way forward is to be decided by the local episcopal authority, or by bishops' conferences, or by the Holy See. Paragraphs 9 and 10 are taken up with the importance of theological study of separated sisters and brothers, and it is stated clearly that future pastors and priests "should have mastered a theology that has been carefully worked out in this way and not controversially, especially with regard to those aspects which concern the relations of separated Christians with the Catholic Church" (paragraph 10). With these words a genuine effort is being made to move beyond the controversial methods of confessional theology that have dominated since the reformations especially of the sixteenth century. Paragraph 11 introduces the important notion of a "hierarchy of truths." This means for a Catholic that not all truths of the faith are on the same level of importance.

29. This is well expressed in Gaillardetz and Clifford, "What Can We Learn?" 152–53.

Chapter 3 of the decree is entitled "Churches and Ecclesial Communities Separated from the Roman Apostolic See." Attention is drawn to the divisions between East and West and then to those normally referred to as "the Reformation." In respect of Reformation traditions we read this statement: "Among those in which Catholic traditions and institutions in part continue to subsist, the Anglican Communion occupies a special place" (paragraph 13). Then paragraphs 14 through 18 are devoted to the special position of the Eastern churches.

> It must not be forgotten that from the beginning the churches of the East have had a treasury from which the Western church has drawn extensively—in liturgical practice, spiritual tradition and canon law. Nor must we undervalue the fact that it was the ecumenical councils held in the East that defined the basic dogmas of the Christian faith, on the Trinity and on the Word of God, who took flesh of the Virgin Mary (paragraph 14).

So much is held in common with the churches of the East. The divisions that separated East from West are complex, but it is stated very clearly that they flow "also from a lack of mutual understanding and charity" (paragraph 14). As paragraph 15 starts out we find once more the centrality of the Eucharist: "Everyone knows with what great love the Christians of the East celebrate the sacred liturgy, especially the Eucharistic mystery, which is the source of the church's life and the pledge of future glory." This centering on the Eucharist enables the recognition that these churches "though separated from us, yet possess true sacraments, above all, by apostolic succession, the priesthood and the Eucharist, whereby they are still linked with us in closest intimacy. Therefore some worship in common, given suitable circumstances and the approval of church authority, is not merely possible but to be encouraged" (paragraph 15). Attention is then given to separated churches and ecclesial communities in the West. Ecumenical relationships with these ecclesial traditions stemming from the Reformation are more difficult not only because of historical, sociological, psychological, and cultural reasons, but also in respect of revealed truth and of Christian doctrine. The council fathers take up their love for Scripture: "Love and reverence, almost a cult, for holy Scripture leads our brothers and sisters to a constant and expert study of the sacred text" (paragraph 21). The sacrament of baptism is acknowledged as establishing a bond between all Christians, but the decree adds that baptism inaugurates the new life in Christ and points to "the completeness of unity which Eucharistic communion gives" (paragraph 22). Yet again, we hear about the centrality of the Eucharist. The council fathers go on to say, however, what everyone knows and what requires great energy in ecumenical commitment:

> Though the ecclesial communities which are separated from us lack the fullness of unity with us which flows from baptism, and though we believe they have not retained the authentic and full reality of the Eucharistic mystery, especially because the sacrament of orders is lacking, nevertheless when they commemorate his death and resurrection in the Lord's supper, they profess that it signifies life in communion with Christ and look forward to his coming in glory. For these reasons dialogue should include among its subjects the Lord's Supper and other sacraments, worship and the church's ministry (paragraph 22).

Needless to point out in the second decade of the third millennium, bilateral and multilateral dialogues on Eucharist and ministry have taken place, as well as in-depth study of the Eucharist on the part of those Christian traditions which traditionally have not held a high sacramental awareness. Suffice it to say at this point that there is an openness to deep ecumenical conversations about the Eucharist and ministry that simply were not there to the same degree before Vatican II. Finally, the decree ends on a note of hope: "It is because of this that the Synod grounds its hope deeply on Christ's prayer for the church, on the Father's love for us, and on the power of the Holy Spirit. 'And hope does not disappoint us, because God's love has been poured into our hearts through the Holy Spirit, who has been given to us' (Romans 5:5)" (paragraph 24). It is fair to say that the council fathers realized that the path towards Christian unity would be a long one, would not be without its challenges and difficulties, but ending on this note of hope sends a very clear message to all Christians concerned with Christian unity today. That message is that hope does not disappoint. There is no room for what has been called "the sin of premature pessimism."[30]

Concluding Reflections

There is a passage from the ecumenical theologian Michael Fahey, SJ that should be required reading for every Catholic:

---

30. The term comes from William H. Lazareth in Horgan, ed., *Walking Together*, 26.

> Acquired habits (especially bad ones) do not easily go away. Some writers, including Catholics still continue to use the term "the church" as a shorthand description for "the Catholic Church," even though it was explicitly stated at the Vatican Council II that the church is a reality broader and more comprehensive than the Roman Catholic Church. Also problematic is the way that some Catholics still say "church" when they intend to designate "the leadership or decision-makers of the Catholic Church." Now that Christians have moved into the third millennium, there is a growing awareness that they must learn to contemplate and conceive the church not just as one's confessional family but as the wider community of all who believe in Christ whose number is known to God alone.[31]

A superb passage; a passage that contains in summary so much of the essence of Vatican II's ecumenical ecclesiology.

There are consequences to this perspective of the council. "Unity" does not mean "uniformity." In other words, whatever final shape church unity will have, it will be a unity that embraces the giftedness of all Christian traditions. An ecclesiology of communion has steadily been gaining ground among the churches and ecclesial communities as well as within the Catholic Church itself. "The category of 'communion' is important in ecumenical discussion for two reasons: first, because it defines the church in terms of those elements of faith and grace that create community rather than ecclesiastical structures; second, because it also allows for degrees of unity among the various churches."[32]

In respect of an ecclesiology of communion, the two fundamental sacraments are baptism and Eucharist. Baptism in the name of the Trinity creates communion. At the same time, traditionally the terminal sacrament of Christian initiation has been the Eucharist. This is why the Eucharist is mentioned several times in the decree, and why it remains such a central part of ecumenical dialogue and understanding.

Some characterize the style of the decree as "triumphal," even as it is conciliatory.[33] There may be some element of truth in that. However, let us agree immediately that there is no room for triumphalism, and let us also recognize simultaneously the importance of maintaining doctrinal and ecclesial traditions firmly, even as we try to reach out with greater

---

31. Fahey, "Ecumenical Ecclesiology," 115.
32. Wood, "Theology of Communion," 103.
33. See, for example, Shannon, "A Free Church Perspective," 34–36.

understanding both to the other and to ourselves. Since the decree was promulgated, and especially since Pope John Paul II's 1994 encyclical letter *That They May Be One*, there can be no disagreement about the importance of ecumenism for Roman Catholics. Furthermore, there is a growing realization or recognition in many Christian quarters that a Petrine primacy—however shaped in response to contemporary and future circumstances—is a ministry needed in the church today, comparable to that of St. Peter in relation to the Twelve.[34] Great strides have been made here.

The ecumenical dialogues recommended and encouraged by the decree have been enormously fruitful. To take but two examples: those of ARCIC—the Anglican-Roman Catholic International Commission and the World Council of Churches' document *Baptism, Eucharist and Ministry* (1982). In 1987, the Vatican Secretariat for Promoting Christian Unity described this latter document as "perhaps the most significant result of the movement so far."[35]

John Henry Newman, the nineteenth-century theologian who spent the first forty-five years of his life as an Anglican and the last forty-five years as a Catholic, somewhere stated that it takes about one hundred years to receive an ecumenical council. We are about the halfway mark in respect of Vatican II and especially its decree and ecumenism. Much that has happened is good. More needs to be done.

---

34. Vogel, "Ecumenism and Challenge," 8. See also Wainwright, *Reformation Over?* especially 49–51.

35. Cited in Dulles, "Decree on Ecumenism," 20.

4

Ecumenical Pioneer, Michael Hurley, SJ (1923–2011)

The division of Christians is for me probably the greatest scandal of the church's history. I am convinced that it is, much more than the vices or mistakes of our societies, the greatest obstacle to evangelization.

Jean M. R. Tillard.[1]

It is the considered unanimous view of all the Churches involved in the ecumenical movement that Christian disunity is a contradiction of the Church's very nature, preventing the Church from being the Church, reducing it steadily to the position in which it is more an obstacle than an instrument of the Spirit, more an enemy than an ally of the Gospel.

Michael Hurley.[2]

---

1. Tillard, *I Believe, Despite Everything*, 15.
2. Hurley, "The Future," in his *Irish Anglicanism 1869–1969*, 211.

Ecumenical Pioneer, Michael Hurley, SJ (1923–2011)

Introduction to Michael Hurley

In July 1995, two theologians, both ecumenical pioneers, received honorary doctorates from Trinity College Dublin, Professor Hans Küng and Fr. Michael Hurley, SJ. Both men were Catholic priests; both were born in the same decade, Küng in 1928 and Hurley in 1923, Küng in Switzerland and Hurley in Ireland. However, Hans Küng became a household name, as it were, throughout the Christian world and Michael Hurley was well known only in Ireland. Arguably, however, Hurley achieved great things ecumenically in Ireland no less than Küng did globally.

If in the words that open this essay, veteran ecumenist Jean Tillard (1927–2000), the late Canadian Dominican, invites us to recognize Christian division as the greatest scandal of the church's history, a sentiment entirely congruent with that of Bishop Lesslie Newbigin, discussed in chapter 2. Like Bishop Newbigin, Michael Hurley, the late Irish Jesuit (1923–2011), demonstrates a life committed to healing that division. He was certainly the pioneer of ecumenism in Ireland, the founder and first director of the Irish School of Ecumenics, now affiliated with Trinity College Dublin.

Following his undergraduate studies in classics at University College Dublin and the study of Scholastic philosophy in the Jesuit program of formation, Hurley proceeded to Louvain (Belgium) for his theology. He found there a genuinely ecumenical approach to theology, not least in bibliographical references in the various theology courses to Protestant and Orthodox authors. This was especially the case with one of his professors, George Dejaifve, SJ, who was very sympathetic to the growing ecumenical movement. In 1954 Hurley was ordained to the priesthood by the then Bishop Léon-Joseph Suenens, later to be Cardinal-Archbishop of Malines and one of the leaders, as we have seen, of Pope John XXIII's Second Vatican Council. His ecumenical appetite had been whetted and he went on to study for a doctorate in theology, awarded by Rome's Gregorian University in 1961. During his time at the Gregorian, he attended a lecture by the famous Anglican ecumenist, Bishop George Bell. Bell had been for many years one of the leading advocates of the ecumenical movement, which, of course, had been greatly energized after the inception of the World Council of Churches in Amsterdam in 1948. Continuing to develop his ecumenical perspective, Hurley's doctoral thesis was on "*Sola Scriptura* and John Wyclif."[3]

---

3. This dissertation was co-published by the Gregorian University and by Fordham

Hurley returned to Ireland to teach at the Jesuit theology faculty of Milltown Park, Dublin. In 1959 the faculty made the decision to hold public lectures in theology, something rather unusual at that time. Hurley suggested as one of the topics "Christian unity." Since no one on the faculty appeared to have any expertise in this area, it fell to him. From that time he says, "I was never allowed to look back."[4] The lecture was delivered on March 9, 1960 and the title was "The Ecumenical Movement."[5]

His first "outside" major ecumenical invitation came from the Anglican professor Frederick Ercolo Vokes, Archbishop King Professor of Divinity at Trinity College Dublin. Vokes's interests were mainly in the New Testament and the patristic period, and he was one of the earliest scholars writing in English to renew interest in the *Didache*.[6] Professor Vokes was also president of the Trinity College branch of the Student Christian Movement, always with a strong ecumenical interest, and it was in that role that he invited Michael Hurley in 1962 to address the branch on the topic "The Vatican Council and the Ecumenical Situation Today." However, there was a problem. Trinity College Dublin was "forbidden territory for Catholics," and so Professor Vokes arranged for him to address the branch off campus in a nearby hotel.[7] From that time on he became a major player—arguably *the* major player—on the ecumenical scene in Ireland. He took part in a variety of ecumenical conferences and plans, continued to publish papers in the area of ecumenical theology, and began to receive recognition in the wider church. His ecumenical participation and his increasing ecumenical collegiality paved the way for his very concise summary of ecumenical theology, *Theology of Ecumenism*, published in 1968.[8] The volume may be slim in terms of its mere ninety-six pages, but the theology that it provides is most impressive, not only for the time in which it was written, but also for today. In the second part of 1968 he prepared his edition of John Wesley's *Letter to a Roman Catholic*, to which reference has been made in chapter 1.

University Press in 1960 as *Scriptura Sola, Wyclif and His Critics*, 1960.

4. Hurley, *Healing and Hope*, 32.

5. This was published as *Towards Christian Unity: An Introduction to the Ecumenical Movement*, 1961.

6. Vokes, *Riddle of the Didache*.

7. Hurley, *Healing and Hope*, 40–41.

8. Hurley, "The Beginnings (1960–1970)," in his *Irish School of Ecumenics*, 29.

ECUMENICAL PIONEER, MICHAEL HURLEY, SJ (1923–2011)

The Irish School of Ecumenics (1970–80)

Writing in 2008, Michael Hurley makes the point emphatically that the reality of Vatican II and rapidly changing circumstances brought about by television and other social media paved the way for the Irish School of Ecumenics.[9] True enough, but the plain fact is that without the initiative, the energy and the commitment of Michael Hurley himself, it never would have happened. The Irish School of Ecumenics has been described by David F. Ford, Regius Professor of Divinity at the University of Cambridge, as "one of the most imaginative and important academic institutional developments in Ireland in the past half century."[10]

In Ireland at the time this inter-denominational school was quite unique. The formal inauguration of the Irish School of Ecumenics took place on November 9, 1970, and the inaugural lecture was given by the General Secretary of the World Council of Churches, Dr. Eugene Carson Blake.[11] It was a thrilling moment for ecumenism in an Ireland torn by sectarian strife. Writing in 2008 and looking back at the history of the Irish School of Ecumenics, Hurley had this to say: "At the beginning we had nothing but goodwill and hope; with these we have risen, if not to glory, at least to be a 'living and life-giving' academic body; we are at least a partial success."[12] This seems to me a typically humble sentiment. Much is dependent, of course, on how one judges success. Placing Michael Hurley in the context of Ireland in the mid-twentieth century and now into the twenty-first, the Irish School of Ecumenics has been and is much more than a partial success. It has firmly and courageously maintained the ecumenical front at a most difficult time in Irish history, and the research topics of its *alumni* as well as their geographical origins show that the ecumenical seeds have been well sown and are producing a rich harvest.

Writing in the Hurley Festschrift in 1993, long-standing Anglican ecumenist Mary Tanner offered these words: "[Michael Hurley's] work for reconciliation has been a beacon in the context of Northern Ireland."[13] Tanner's words make reference to Hurley's participation in the Columbanus

---

9. Ibid., 27–28.
10. Ford, "Foreword," 16.
11. Eugene Carson Blake (1906–85) was General Secretary of the WCC from 1966–74.
12. Hurley, "Preface," in his *Irish School of Ecumenics*, 8.
13. Tanner, "Towards Visible Unity," 20, slightly adapted.

Community of Reconciliation in Belfast in Northern Ireland, in which he lived and witnessed in a very practical way to the ecumenical cause from 1983–93. The idea for the Columbanus Community of Reconciliation came to Hurley in 1981. "Its aim was rather to challenge the sectarianism, injustice and violence prevalent in Northern Ireland and elsewhere in our world, to do so in deed not just in word, to give a practical example of integrated living, of what a more united church, a more just society and a more peaceful world could be like, to give encouragement to those committed to an improvement in interchurch relations."[14] The residential community prayed regularly together, celebrated the Eucharist daily but without eucharistic sharing, and the members often worked in the local community. They were a living sign in Belfast that Catholics and Protestants could live together, pray together, without rancor even as they had their differences of belief and practice. The Community unfortunately closed in 2002. The reasons had to do in the main with declining residential membership and financial support. It was also about this time that Michael Hurley was diagnosed with cancer. He was to live for almost another decade.

In retirement Hurley gave retreats and continued to preach, especially in an ecumenical context. In 1998 he published a collection of his articles over the decades entitled *Christian Unity: An Ecumenical Second Spring?* Close to the beginning of that work he indicates his intention: "Its aim is to make some modest contribution towards ensuring that the third millennium does in fact bring an ecumenical second Spring . . . ."[15] A former student and good friend of Michael Hurley at the Irish School of Ecumenics, Fintan Lyons, has written this of him: "His greatest achievement at the public level was his founding of the Irish School of Ecumenics and perhaps the greatest tribute to him is that the growth and development of this institution in the present has occurred while its founder remains in the shadowy past, hardly to be mentioned."[16] This is probably what ecumenical leaders and theologians should expect, that is to say, that as the movement towards greater Christian unity moves forward, they fade into the background, "hardly to be mentioned." The legacy of ecumenists' work and commitment will go on until the goal is reached, however inchoate that goal may be at this time and whenever in the future.

---

14. Hurley, *Healing and Hope*, 71.
15. Hurley, *Christian Unity*, 6.
16. Lyons, "Healing and Hope," 261.

Ecumenical Pioneer, Michael Hurley, SJ (1923–2011)

Theology of Ecumenism

Now it is time to turn to Michael Hurley's very fine little book entitled *Theology of Ecumenism* published in 1969, just four years after the close of Vatican II in 1965.[17] He presents his understanding of ecumenism in the light of the Council's Decree on Ecumenism and in the light of texts and documents that had emerged in the course of the century especially from the World Council of Churches.

In the introduction Hurley wrote these words: "Once upon a time Roman Catholics thought of ecumenism as something external and indeed alien to Catholicism, about which we ought of course to be well-informed—in order the better to resist and refute it—and towards which we might perhaps be sympathetic but with which we emphatically had nothing whatsoever to do: ecumenism was for 'them' not for us."[18] He rightly notes—and it seems as true now in many ways as it did in 1969—that our ways of thinking and acting vis-à-vis other Christians is marked by, or perhaps better marred by our instinct for self-preservation and indeed, our aggressiveness. As a result, "we cling more fiercely than ever to our old identities, to the myth of our incommunicable otherness."[19] To counter these understandable fears he counsels personal involvement. "Action does lead to understanding, and to go with a friend to an ecumenical conference will do much more for us than reading any number of books, this one included."[20] While fear of the Christian other is acknowledged by Hurley as a real barrier to Christian unity, he believes that disillusionment is a much more formidable issue. Disillusionment, perhaps especially among the young, may arise from seeing the ecumenical movement "as a dying institution's indecent grasping after lost power and prestige," or perhaps also from a suspicion of clericalism, triumphalism, and verbalism.[21] Hurley's analysis, brief as it is, seems to me to speak as much to the present situation as it did at the time of his writing. In order to counteract the impediments to ecumenism, Hurley strongly recommends what he describes as the "ecumenizing" of theological education. His reasoning is clear. If those who are preparing to minister in the church do not possess a solid grasp of the principles of ecumenism

---

17. Hurley, *Theology of Ecumenism*.
18. Ibid., 9.
19. Ibid., 10.
20. Ibid., 11.
21. Ibid., 12.

and are not committed to the cause, then those whom they are destined to serve in the various Christian traditions can hardly be expected to develop ecumenical mindedness.

Hurley insists on the missionary dimension of the Christian church. "The fundamental principle of ecumenism is that the nature of the church is to be a missionary church, that Christianity is essentially missionary, that its unity is for mission and its disunity therefore a scandal and a stumbling block."[22] Here Hurley is pointing to the documents of Vatican II, and especially the Decree on the Missionary Activity of the Church which states that "the pilgrim church is missionary by her very nature."[23] Though he would not in all probability have known it at the time, Hurley was also echoing the ecclesiological point of view of Bishop Lesslie Newbigin, of the Church of South India, discussed in chapter 2. The church as mission follows from the mission of the Son, sent by the Father so that, in the Johannine phrase, "the world may believe." "The church therefore is sent to be the sacrament, the efficacious sign, of the unity of mankind and of the salvation of the world."[24] Disunity among Christians works against the very *raison d'être* of the church. "To the degree in which the church is disunited it loses its secret mysterious power of speaking to the hearts of men, of challenging their selfishness, of enlarging their vision, of liberating and enhancing their energies for the service of God and the world."[25] Hurley does not mince his words. He has the firm and clear conviction that the church cannot be mission without the simultaneous commitment to Christian unity, and if this is not in place then the church will die. He writes: "There are unfortunately many Christians who still remain deaf to this message of the Spirit, who do not yet realize that the churches must dialogue or the Church will die: die as event, as the sacramental presence of the event of salvation." And he reiterates his equally passionate conviction that this commitment must be fueled by not only prayer, the great contribution of the Abbé Couturier, but also by theological education.[26] Hurley was consistently emphatic about the latter. This is no Pelagian approach to ecumenism for Hurley because he insists no less emphatically on the intrinsic connection between liturgy and mission. Although he does not quite develop it in this fashion, he seems to imply

22. Ibid., 22.
23. Paragraph 2.
24. Hurley, *Theology of Ecumenism*, 23.
25. Ibid.
26. Ibid., 24.

that the liturgical assembly, as the Body of Christ, deepened and strengthened as the Body of Christ through the Eucharist, must be as Christ was, that is to say, in mission.[27]

As he charts his way across the ecumenical map, as it were, Hurley is acutely aware also of the non-theological, or the non-doctrinal impediments to church unity. In this regard he cites the sentiments of a nineteenth-century Roman Catholic bishop in Ireland, Bishop James of Kildare and Leighlin:

> The existing diversity of opinions arises, in most cases, from certain forms of words which admit of satisfactory explanation, or from ignorance and misconceptions which ancient prejudice and ill will produce and strengthen, but which could be removed; they are pride and points of honor which keep us divided on many subjects, not a love of Christian humility, charity and truth.[28]

He notes that prior to the establishment of the World Council of Churches, the Second World Conference on Faith and Order at Edinburgh in 1937 made the same point quite sharply speaking of obstacles to Christian unity that have to do with barriers of nationality, race, class, and general culture. In 1952, he notes again that the Third World Conference on Faith and Order at Lund witnessed the following comments by one of the speakers: "Students of religion have long known that culture, social structure and habits, climate, economic conditions, forms of government, national loyalties and the like affect all religions *except their own*."[29] Hurley italicizes the last three words and with good reason. It is a sociological fact that many institutions have as a top priority their own self-perpetuation. In and out of this ingrained habit of self-preservation arises the faculty of perceiving problems in others, but not in oneself. This too is as true today as it was when Hurley was writing. The ecumenical movement cannot succeed—however its goal is finally articulated—if the Christian churches and traditions do not recognize their own indigenous need for change and development, not least in these non-doctrinal spheres. Vatican II's Decree on Ecumenism acknowledges this in paragraphs 9, 14, and 19. Hurley, however, finds it regrettable that the decree did not give more emphasis to these non-doctrinal factors. Turning to the Council of Florence in the fifteenth century, as well as to our contemporary places of tension that have more to do with non-doctrinal

---

27. Ibid., 25–28.
28. Ibid., 29.
29. Ibid., 31.

factors than with theological divisions Hurley writes as follows: "The whole religious situation in Greece, Scotland, Ireland and many other places seriously challenges this interpretation (of non-doctrinal factors being secondary in importance)."[30] In respect of Greece he points to the situation of the monastic communities of Mount Athos as an illustration of the too close identification of the Orthodox Church with nationalism and an anti-Romanism, something Hurley himself experienced in later life when on pilgrimage there. In respect of Ireland, while he was writing before the explosion of violence and terrorism in the 1970s and 1980s, he had a clear realization of these non-doctrinal factors and, indeed, of their volatility. He writes:

> In Ireland too doctrinal differences are patently insufficient by themselves to explain the existing divisions and tensions. Despite our desires and efforts to escape from the bondage of the past, centuries of unfortunate historical associations still prevent the achievement of religious unity, still mark inter-church relations with fear and bitterness and bigotry, with a pride and prejudice, and arrogance and antipathy which can be satisfactorily understood only in terms of "old, unhappy, far-off things and battles long ago."[31]

Prescient words when one considers what took place in the years to follow in Ireland. Ecumenism needs to be done and needs to be seen to be done not only in terms of mission, but as love, love for the other whatever tradition the other stands for. He cited some words from John Wesley's *Letter to a Roman Catholic*: "I think you deserve the tenderest regard I can show. . . . If we cannot as yet think alike in all things, at least we may love alike." "Ecumenism is love because love is the only possible solvent of our disunity such as it is. Only love is capable of casting out fear and bitterness and bigotry, of overcoming arrogance and antipathy, of neutralizing the assets of rancor and resentment, of transcending the various non-doctrinal issues which prevent us from obeying God's will for the missionary unity of his people."[32]

As he continues with this understanding of the principles of ecumenism, Hurley goes on to comment on a very famous phrase and change that occurred in Vatican II's Constitution on the Church, paragraph 8: "The

---

30. Ibid., 31–32.

31. Ibid., 33. See also in this regard the fine work of Irish Methodist theologian William J. Abraham, *Shaking Hands with the Devil*.

32. Hurley, *Theology of Ecumenism*, 34.

unique Church of Christ... subsists in the Catholic Church." He recognizes that the verb "subsists" replaces the verb "is," found in the original draft of the document. This seemingly small and insignificant verbal change is, in point of fact, of great theological importance. Here is its importance as stated by Hurley: "The Roman Catholic Church is no longer claimed to be absolutely identical with the Church of the Creed."[33] That being the case, its recognition and acceptance means that Christians in different ecclesial traditions are closer to each other than many might imagine. It also demands that "we must stress what we have in common rather than what separates us, that we all belong, though in varying degrees, to the one true Church."[34] In a fine paragraph Hurley provides further commentary on this point that speaks to the sensibilities of Catholics. He points out that even among Catholics differentiations about being in full communion are both implicit and explicit:

> We know that full initiation into the Church calls for baptism, confirmation and the Eucharist; that in consequence those who have not yet received the latter two sacraments do not yet belong fully to the Church, are not yet in full communion with it. We also know that the Roman Catholic who is in a state of mortal sin has to be reconciled to the Church as well as to God; that, in consequence, he lacks not only full invisible communion with God but also full visible communion with the Church, so that we forbid him, as in general we forbid Protestants, access to the Eucharist; that he too like Protestants stands in need of formal reconciliation; that he does indeed belong to the Church but only imperfectly and partially.[35]

The point is worth dwelling on at some length, even as it sounds like something very minor. Hurley puts it very succinctly: "The effective valid baptism, whenever and by whomsoever administered, is to incorporate the recipient into the Church, not into the Presbyterian or Methodist or Anglican Church but into the Church of the Creed, into the one true Church."[36] In brief, Christians have so very much in common. In this regard Hurley cites the church historian and Newman biographer Meriol Trevor, a convert from agnosticism to Catholicism: "As an ex-agnostic, I must express

---

33. Ibid., 40.
34. Ibid.
35. Ibid., 41.
36. Ibid.

my permanent surprise that people who have been Christians all their lives can get so excited over their differences, which are so very small (yes, *small*) beside the enormous difference between believing in Christ and not believing in him."³⁷

In very practical terms this demands of Christians an avoidance and renunciation of proselytism. That principle may be found in Vatican II's Declaration on Religious Freedom, paragraph 4: "In spreading religious faith and in introducing religious practices, everyone ought at all times to refrain from any manner of action which might seem to carry a hint of coercion or of a kind of persuasion that would be dishonorable or unworthy, especially when dealing with poor or uneducated people. Such a manner of action would have to be considered an abuse of one's own right and a violation of the right of others." Proselytism is, of course, quite different from evangelization. Evangelization is simply the church-as-mission proclaiming its message. Christians who wish to take the initiative and to change their ecclesial allegiance must be free to do so. At the same time, there must be no element of coercion or dishonorable persuasion. To say the least, this way of understanding requires a much more careful and sensitive form of expression, especially among Roman Catholics. Roman Catholics have a long-established tendency of describing other Christians as "entering into the church," or some such phrase. This way of expression needs correction especially because other Christians who become Roman Catholics are already baptized, and as baptized persons are already and really church. When such persons decide to become Roman Catholics what is happening is that "they are reconciled rather and brought into full communion with [the Roman Catholic Church]." They are not entering the church, but being brought into full communion with the church.³⁸ Hurley concludes in this fashion: for such persons "Our aim, however, will be to help them, not to help ourselves. Our aim will be their spiritual good, not our own numerical advancement; and their spiritual good will not always and necessarily involve changing their Church allegiance."³⁹

As he opens his final chapter in his *Theology of Ecumenism*, Hurley stresses the importance of hope, active hope in the pursuit of Christian unity: "A pessimistic attitude to ecumenism is so widespread among Christians that

---

37. *The Church Times*, March 12, 1965, cited in Hurley, *Theology of Ecumenism*, 42–43. For some brief context for this quite extraordinary church historian, Meriol Trevor, see Cummings, *Prophets, Guardians and Saints*, v–viii.

38. Hurley, *Theology of Ecumenism*, 50–51.

39. Ibid., 52.

it might well be considered the greatest obstacle to the cause of reconciling the Churches and the clearest sign of the evil and sinfulness of our disunity. In various ways this pessimism provides an excuse for the indifferent, a difficulty for the interested and a temptation for the committed. . . . Even the committed ecumenist finds it hard at times to escape from this black mood of pessimism."[40] If this was true fifty years ago, it is certainly no less true now.

Conclusion

In the "Introduction" to the Festschrift in honor of Michael Hurley, the editor, church historian Oliver Rafferty, SJ, commented on Hurley's ecumenical witness: "It has been at times a thankless task, and clearly there were moments when Fr. Hurley's must have seemed like a voice crying in the wilderness. However his dogged persistence and perseverance have produced results which are a tribute to his singleness of purpose and his ecumenical vocation."[41] Dogged persistence and perseverance are necessary marks of the ecumenist. Progress is never easily measured, and seldom easily experienced by those engaged in the cause of Christian unity. The progress made in the cause of Christian unity in Ireland in the twentieth century and indeed into our present century would simply not have been possible without the personal commitment of Michael Hurley. Yes, ecumenical events and projects would have gone on. But Hurley's growing commitment to the cause, and perhaps especially by the establishment of the Irish School of Ecumenics, are the clearest mile markers of what ecumenical progress there has been. "There is no shortage of ecumenical achievements for want of which the memory and work of Fr. Michael Hurley will fade from the corporate memory of the Christian community in Ireland."[42] Adrian Empey, Anglican priest-historian, states the obvious in these words. The ecumenical witness of Michael Hurley will live long in Ireland and through his many students and colleagues elsewhere far beyond Ireland, not least in the United States. The Italian theologian and now Archbishop Bruno Forte once encouraged Christians in these words: "Live with a passion for the unity of the body of Christ, committing yourself to the search for full communion with all believers in him, and accept religious diversity with

40. Ibid., 86–87.
41. Rafferty, "Introduction," in his *Reconciliation: Essays in Honor of Michael Hurley*, 16.
42. Empey, "Foreword," 14.

respect, promoting dialogue and collaboration with all believers in God, whatever faith they belong to!"[43] Michael Hurley's life and witness inspires other Christians in this third millennium of Christianity to live with a passion for the unity of the body of Christ.

43. Forte, *Essence of Christianity*, 92.

5

John Macquarrie, Church, and Ecumenism

Anglicans consistently define themselves as both Catholic and reformed.

PAUL AVIS.[1]

Today what is at issue is, quite simply, the catholicity of Anglicanism. Are we to be part of the church catholic, or are we to devolve in North America, to two more sects, only with vestments?

GEORGE SUMNER.[2]

Century of the Church

There can be no doubt that the ecclesiological and ecumenical contributions of Michael Hurley would not have been possible without the breakthrough achieved by Vatican II and its Decree on Ecumenism. Arguably, something

---

1. Avis, *Identity of Anglicanism*, 66.
2. Sumner, "After Dromatine," 561.

similar may be said of one of the most important Anglican theologians of the twentieth century, John Macquarrie (1919–2008).[3]

While the opening comment of Paul Avis speaks to Anglican ecclesial self-understanding, that of George Sumner is speaking directly to the somewhat polarized situation of the Episcopal Church in the United States. Sumner is right—the catholicity of Anglicanism in the United States is at issue, but it is equally important not to forget the amazing advances in ecclesiology across the ecumenical frontiers in this century. This century has been described by Otto Dibelius as the "century of the Church."[4] Behind this remark lies the ecumenical movement, which got under way after the Edinburgh Missionary Conference in 1910, paving the way for the establishment of the World Council of Churches in Amsterdam in 1948. The renewal of ecclesiology in the Catholic Church is another factor in the making of this ecclesial century, a renewal fueled by Vatican Council II, especially its Constitution on the Church and Decree on Ecumenism. With the publication of these documents the Catholic Church moved into the ecumenical movement, and has remained committed to it ever since.

As Vatican II moved to its conclusion in 1965, John Macquarrie moved from the Presbyterianism in which he had been brought up and in which he had ministered to the Anglican Communion. This took place while he was teaching at Union Theological Seminary in New York. He had felt the attraction of the Episcopal Church, as the Anglican Communion is known in Scotland, from his youth, and he tells us that "Back in Scotland, and for family reasons, it was difficult for me to break away from the prevailing Presbyterianism and I had been a Presbyterian minister since 1944."[5] In 1965 he was ordained a priest in the Anglican Communion. During this New York period he had also readied his *Principles of Christian Theology* in which he provides an account of his ecclesiology, an ecclesiology that obviously reflected his new ecclesial allegiance. In 1975 he followed this with *Christian Unity and Christian Diversity*, in which he treated of ecumenism and ecumenical theology. Using these books as our primary sources we shall present an account of Macquarrie's ecclesiology. The one thing that is immediately noticeable about Macquarrie's ecclesiology is that it does not indulge in narcissism, an introversion of the church upon itself that

---

3. For a brief introduction to John Macquarrie and his ecclesiology, see Cummings, *John Macquarrie*.

4. Cited in McPartlan, *Sacrament of Salvation*, xiii.

5. Macquarrie, *On Being a Theologian*, 38.

can all too easily slide into place. Macquarrie has no time for that kind of ecclesiology. His ecclesiology describes a church that is connected with the world, that is not self-seeking, and that attempts to engage with difficult questions honestly. For these reasons, it is particularly difficult to understand why the ecclesiological work of John Macquarrie has not featured significantly in contemporary Anglican theology. For example, neither Daniel W. Hardy in his *Finding the Church* (2001),[6] nor Paul Avis in his *The Identity of Anglicanism*, noted above, adverts to the work of Macquarrie.[7] Of course, it is not necessary that they should consider his contribution, but both his prominence in Anglican systematic theology generally and his particular contributions to ecclesiology and to ecumenism seem to warrant some mention.

It is not easy to define with precision what the late Anglican philosophical theologian Daniel W. Hardy (1930–2007) is up to in his essay, "John Macquarrie's Ecclesiology."[8] Hardy always had a real concern for the doing of theology and for the doing of theology in and for the church. In this essay he points out the Cinderella status of ecclesiology (along with liturgy and ethics) in British universities. However, he notes that even in Macquarrie's earliest work on Bultmann and Heidegger, *An Existentialist Theology*, Macquarrie critiques Bultmann for the decided lack of an ecclesial perspective, and as he moved to New York and then to Oxford, he acknowledges that Macquarrie grew in awareness of ecclesiological issues. But these issues were always understood as elements of *practical* theology, as, for example, in the treatment of the church in *Principles of Christian Theology*. Hardy writes: "All these institutional settings (in Macquarrie's case Glasgow, New York, Oxford) have one thing in common: they make ecclesiology a matter for practical, rarely doctrinal, concern."[9] What would it mean to make ecclesiology a matter of doctrinal concern? Reading between Hardy's lines it seems to be the case for him that ecclesiology should flow out of Christian doctrine and, although he is not explicit he seems to intend such doctrines as Trinity and incarnation, and thus be treated on a par with them, entirely integrated with them, rather than be regarded as

---

6. Hardy, *Finding the Church*.

7. In the case of Daniel Hardy, the omission of Macquarrie is particularly striking. Hardy was thoroughly familiar with Macquarrie's theology.

8. In the 2006 celebration of Macquarrie's theology, *In Search of Humanity and Deity*, 267–76.

9. Hardy, "John Macquarrie's Ecclesiology," 269.

a practical consequence of them. On this particular point Hardy is in line with the best and longest of the Christian tradition of theological reflection. His criticism of Macquarrie, similar to his criticism noted in chapter 1, is that Macquarrie starts from human experience in general, not specifically Christian experience. This being so, Macquarrie's starting-point for theology cannot explicitly be ecclesiological. Macquarrie's approach to theology is experiential-reflective and Hardy finds the experiential-reflective starting-point problematic, probably (but not explicitly) in line with George Lindbeck's critique of experiential-expressivism in theology.[10] Hardy writes:

> Furthermore, as widespread as it is in theology and theological education, there is a problem with the experiential-reflective mode of theological reasoning. Reflection is always *posterior* to experience, and *prior* to further experience. It is a "moment" after and before experience when experience is correlated with theological reflection, which . . . is usually so generalized as to be disconnected from experience. In other words, even the best theological reflection loses touch with the particularities of experience.[11]

Does Hardy have reflection right here? As human persons develop, they develop always in an environment that is already interpreted, or reflected, in some tradition or another. However, they always reflect as both the inheritor of a tradition and as the contributor, in some fashion, to that tradition. To speak of reflection as a moment after and before experience does not seem to be the case, and certainly does not seem to reflect adequately the position behind Macquarrie's theology and ecclesiology.

The Church in Relation to Other Christian Doctrines

All of Christian doctrine is inter-connected, so that to engage with one doctrine is inevitably to find oneself engaged with another, and ultimately with the entire fabric of Christian teaching. In this vein Macquarrie sees the church knit into other doctrines, and arguably deals with ecclesiology

---

10. See Lindbeck, *The Nature of Doctrine*, and the appreciative assessment of Lindbeck in Cummings, "Toward a Postliberal Religious Education," 315–24. While I stand by much of what is written in this essay on Lindbeck, even then and much more now I feel that he is philosophically flawed when it comes to the role of philosophy in theology. It is no surprise that in Lindbeck's collection of essays *The Church in a Postliberal Age*, there is no reference to John Macquarrie.

11. Hardy, "John Macquarrie's Ecclesiology," 275.

in terms of doctrinal concern, *pace* Hardy. First, the church must be understood in relation to the doctrine of creation. "The Church is already implicit in creation."[12] The church is there in the beginning, from the beginning. There has always been a community of faith in the world, "as far back as we can go," well captured in Hebrews 11:4–7. In that sense the entire human race constitutes the people of God, but "this does not detract from the need for a special group, a special people whose destiny and service it is to realize and to represent an authentic existence for all. . . . [The church] is the spearhead of what is going on in the creation as a whole."[13]

Moving towards the doctrine of the incarnation, the church finds its most distinctive title as the "body of Christ" (1 Cor 12:27; Eph 1:23; Col 1:18). The church, those "in Christ," are being "conformed to christhood, as they participate in the paschal mystery. The church is those who are re-created in Christ, so that it becomes in John Knox's words 'the historical embodiment of the new humanity.'"[14] In this light, one may speak of the church legitimately as the "extension" of the incarnation, though care must be taken not to mistake the church in its complete and final condition. "The incarnation which reached its completion in [Christ] is in process in the Church. Our hope is indeed that it is moving toward completion in the Church too, but at any given time, the Church is a mixed body. It is not free from sin, and there may even be times when it slips back."[15]

The doctrine of "the last things" comes next. The church is not be identified with the kingdom of God without qualification, but nor can it be simply distinguished from the kingdom. "We may think of the kingdom as the entelechy of the Church, the perfect unfolding of the potentialities that are already manifesting themselves in the Church."[16] The church is the anticipation of the kingdom, or one might say the sacrament of the kingdom.

---

12. Macquarrie, *Principles*, 386.

13. Ibid., 388, 407.

14. John Knox was Macquarrie's friend and colleague at Union Theological Seminary in New York City. Macquarrie quotes this phrase from Knox's book, *The Church and the Reality of Christ*, 104.

15. Macquarrie, *Principles*, 389.

16. Ibid., 390.

The Marks of the Church

The four traditional marks of the church are unity, holiness, catholicity, and apostolicity. "The Christian hope is that these notes will come through more and more clearly as the Church moves towards its consummation."[17] The first note of the church is unity, the center of which is Jesus Christ himself. Since Christ is the head of the body, the church, he is the source of that body's unity. The unity of the body, however, is not to be identified with uniformity. Macquarrie underscores the insight of St. Paul that unity and diversity go together, as in that wonderful passage of 1 Corinthians 12. The challenge is to maintain unity and diversity in a fine balance, eschewing both uniformity and autonomy, and the key is the doctrine of the holy Trinity. In the Trinity the unity of God is expressed in the three persons of the Trinity: "The ultimate model for the Church's unity is therefore the unity of the triune God, a unity embracing the richest diversity and thus one in which there is neither stifling absorption nor damaging division."[18]

Perhaps we can see here an ecclesiology of communion in Macquarrie, communion being a central ecclesiological concept in contemporary theology. "Communion" clearly does not have the developed place in Macquarrie's ecclesiology that it enjoys in today's ecumenical reflection on the church. One thinks, for example, of the influential work of the Greek Orthodox theologian, Metropolitan John D. Zizioulas and the Catholic Jean M. R. Tillard, OP. In both of these authors, communion is a key category for understanding the church.[19] This is missing in Macquarrie, at least as an explicit, ecumenical, ecclesiological, category. However, insofar as communion is seen to be ecclesial participation in the life of the Trinity, and one recognizes that it is more nuanced than this bald statement would lead one to believe, then this is reflected in Macquarrie's thought.

The second note of the church is holiness. Holiness means "being an agent of the incarnation, letting Christ be formed in the Church and in the world."[20] This formation of Christ that is both ecclesial and cosmic in scope is always partial and unfulfilled before the parousia. The church is always the church *in via*, on the way. It is a church in the pellucid phrase of

---

17. Ibid., 402.

18. Ibid., 403. The same point is made in Macquarrie, *Christian Unity and Diversity*, 47.

19. Zizioulas, *Being as Communion*, and Tillard, *Church of Churches*.

20. Macquarrie, *Principles*, 405.

Aidan Nichols, OP, echoing an Augustinian emphasis, in which sinners "are hospitalized . . . with a view to being made well, and made saints."[21]

Catholicity is the third note of the church, and it includes two distinct but related ideas. First, is the notion of "universality." The church is for all people everywhere, transcending all cultures. "It is this inclusive unity-in-diversity that constitutes the catholicity of the church as universality."[22] Secondly, catholicity also means authenticity, "authenticity of belief and practice in the church." The authentic faith is learned from the church as a whole, from the universal church, and so this second sense of catholicity is related to the first. Councils of the church, expressive of the consensus of the faithful, is a primary measure of catholicity, for example, in giving rise to the creeds of Christianity, formulated under the guidance of the Holy Spirit. The catholicity of the church in this double sense preserves the church from the dangers of insularity and even ethnocentrism on the one hand, and from loss of identity on the other.

The final mark of the church is apostolicity. It consists in "the church's own living continuity with the apostles."[23] Macquarrie draws a helpful analogy for apostolicity with the development of the self: "As the commitment of faith plays an important part in unifying a self, so that we can recognize it as the same self as it moves through time, so too the community of faith is united by the same faith that has spanned the centuries. The formulations of that faith have changed and will change, but the existential attitude which constitutes the core of the faith, has remained constant."[24] The obvious question now is, "How is apostolicity maintained in practice?" The answer is for Macquarrie that the episcopate is the institutional form that protects apostolicity. "This office, publicly transmitted by the apostles to their successors and then on through the generations, is the overt, institutional vehicle for ensuring the continuity of that heritage of faith and practice which was likewise transmitted by the apostles."[25] Macquarrie finds himself in agreement with his Union Theological Seminary colleague, John Knox, when he says, "I for one have no hesitancy in ascribing the same status to episcopacy as to canon and creed."[26] Historically, the church exhibits these

21. Nichols, *Epiphany*, 237.
22. Macquarrie, *Principles*, 407.
23. Ibid., 409.
24. Ibid., 410.
25. Ibid.
26. Ibid., 411.

four marks in a "more or less" fashion until it reaches its completion in the kingdom of God.

The Petrine Ministry

Macquarrie's views of the Petrine ministry have undergone considerable development over the course of his theological career. Writing an Anglican reply in 1970 to the question, "What Still Separates us from the Catholic Church?" Macquarrie insists along with most members of the Anglican Communion that the Anglican Communion does not consider itself *separate* from the Catholic Church: "Anglicanism has never considered itself to be a sect or denomination originating in the sixteenth century. It continues without a break the *Ecclesia Anglicana* founded by St. Augustine thirteen centuries and more ago, though nowadays that branch of the church has spread far beyond the borders of England." The question is better formulated in this way: "What still separates Anglicans and Romans *within* the Catholic Church to which they so visibly and manifestly belong?"[27] Responding to the question thus phrased, Macquarrie went on to give his attention to the papacy and it has remained a published interest of his. "At the very least, we have to affirm that any vision of a reunited church, one, holy, catholic and apostolic, must envisage it in communion with the most illustrious of the apostolic sees. Anything short of this can be regarded only as an interim step; and anything that might make this ultimate consummation more difficult should be scrupulously avoided."[28] Thus does Macquarrie begin his first treatment of the papacy in his *Principles*.

The New Testament in his judgment makes clear the special status, the primacy of St. Peter among the apostles: his recognition of Jesus as Messiah (Mark 8:29); Christ's declaration that he was the rock on which he will build the church (Matt. 16:18); he was the first of the apostles to see the risen Christ (1 Cor 15:5, etc.); and it is to Peter that the risen Christ commends the care of the church in the Gospel of John (John 21:15–19); in the Acts of the Apostles Peter acts as a spokesman for the church; Peter is the first to open the church to the Gentiles; even when Paul has a disagreement with Peter, he makes it abundantly clear that he acknowledges the special

---

27. Macquarrie's essay may be found in Hans Küng, ed., *Post-Ecumenical Christianity*, here 45–46.
28. Macquarrie, *Principles*, 416.

place Peter has in the church.[29] Though there are historical obscurities in the post-apostolic church about the development of the Petrine ministry, Macquarrie does not see this as a significant problem. Rather, the same kind of obscurity obtains in respect of the rise of the New Testament canon, the development of the sacraments, and the emergence of the threefold shape of ministry (diaconate, presbyterate, episcopate). "If we are to call the latter three apostolic, should we deny the title to the papacy?"[30] Just as these agencies have been instrumental in nurturing the unity and integrity if the church, so has the papacy.

The central problematic issue with the papacy for Macquarrie is infallibility. He admits a basic meaning to the doctrine, a freedom from error, the quality of indefectibility:

> For what is freedom from error if it is not penetration into truth? Could we say that just as a compass needle, when distracting influences have been removed, turns unfailingly toward the north, so the mind of the church, when fully open to the Holy Spirit, turns unfailingly toward the truth?[31]

Indefectibility, thus understood, is not infallibility. Indefectibility is for him an eschatological idea, "but when we talk of 'infallibility,' we are asking about the kind of guidance available to the church *in via*."[32] The doctrine of infallibility implies that "given certain carefully specified conditions . . . on a particular occasion and on a particular matter one can assert that the Pope (or the church) has made a pronouncement that is guaranteed to be free from error."

Writing in 1975, Macquarrie judged this doctrine to be such a formidable obstacle that "[he did] not see any way in which this doctrine could ever become acceptable to Anglicans and Protestants."[33] This description is in his own words "in very negative terms."[34] In his later essay, "The Papacy in a Unified Church," Macquarrie comes to a more positive judgment on infallibility based on the insights of the late Bishop Christopher But-

---

29. These last three notes about Peter come from Macquarrie, *On Being a Theologian*, 163–64.

30. Macquarrie, *Principles*, 413.

31. Ibid., 415. This is a favorite analogy for Macquarrie. He returns to it again in *On Being a Theologian*, 170.

32. Macquarrie, "Structures of Unity," 126.

33. Macquarrie, *Christian Unity and Diversity*, 99–100.

34. Macquarrie, *On Being a Theologian*, 169.

ler—two insights in particular.[35] First, Butler maintained that any verbal expression is necessarily involved in the fallibilities of language, so that, as a result, it may be "inadequate, misleading, and even trailing clouds (of culturally derived error)." This allays some of Macquarrie's anxiety about any linguistic formula being utterly free of error. Butler emphasized that one ought to look at the governing intention behind the term. The actual term "infallibility" is a negative term, that is to say, "it seems to stress the negative notion of inerrancy, whereas what is really at stake is guaranteed truth—a positive notion." Macquarrie still has some difficulty with the expression "guaranteed truth," but recognizes behind it the pneumatological conviction that the Holy Spirit will lead the church into the fullness of truth, using his analogy of the magnetic needle. At the same time, he also accepts that this infallibility, a gift to the whole church, may be exercised in a special way by "the one who leads the church." This leadership, however, must be seen in a corporate or collegial context.[36] Understood in this fashion the dogma of papal infallibility may make sense to Christians not in full communion with Rome.

Invited to comment on Macquarrie's essay, "The Papacy in a Unified Church," the Irish systematic theologian, Eamonn Conway, rightly suggests that the Catholic understanding of infallibility, though very close to his point of view, actually goes further than Macquarrie. He also uses the analogy of the magnetic needle to good effect to establish his point: "the doctrine of papal infallibility claims that, at *particular* decisive moments on its journey the Christian community can be assured that the compass needle is not under any distracting influences and is, in fact, pointing north."[37] But, having said that, Conway insists that, given the stricture that all human language is conditioned by circumstances, noted by Butler and accepted by Macquarrie, "even a defined doctrine is open to development not just in terms of its formulation but also in terms of its content."

The indefectible relation to truth pertains to the whole church and its leadership. In this way Macquarrie sees the role and function of the papacy within the episcopate, as having a primacy *within* the episcopate: "a papacy truly integrated with the bishops and eventually with the whole people of God. The Pope is a sacramental person, an embodiment of the whole

---

35. Macquarrie finds particularly helpful Bishop Christopher Butler's "Roman Requirements," 99–100.

36. Macquarrie, *On Being a Theologian*, 170–71.

37. Conway, "The Papacy in a Pilgrim Church," 175.

church, but he is nothing apart from the church."[38] This is Macquarrie's version of what Vatican Council II called "collegiality," a collegiality that he sees first expressed in the apostolic period: "the scriptural record seems to visualize the leadership of Peter, but it is not a monarchical leadership, but one exercised in consultation with colleagues."[39]

Perhaps, when all is said and done, the nub of the issue is raised well by Bishop Mark Santer, formerly Bishop of Birmingham in England: "In what does the Petrine ministry essentially consist? How far does it entail a function of government?"[40] Macquarrie does not quite raise the question of the papacy in this way, but it is the practical issues implicit in Santer's question that proves particularly problematic. Santer acknowledges, just as Macquarrie would have, that "there is no problem about seeing the Petrine office as a focus for unity," but the issue is whether that ministry really entails the active involvement of the Pope in the government of other churches "such as is exercised today." He allies himself with the perspective of Cardinal Walter Kasper who argues that it is not so much the actual dogma of the First Vatican Council that is problematic as much as its "maximizing interpretation."[41] How is this maximizing interpretation to be avoided, especially in respect of those ecclesial traditions stemming from the sixteenth-century Reformation, traditions that have *a priori* rejected this Petrine ministry? Bishop Santer rightly believes that the response to this question lies in the notion of reception.

> Lurking here is the sensitive issue of reception and what has come to be called re-reception (a word I first learned from the late Fr. Jean Tillard). Anglicans have made it absolutely clear that for them the recognition of the infallibility, freedom from error or irreversibility of any authoritative statement of faith, whether conciliar or primatial, is inseparable from its reception by the church.

He knows the formulas of the First Vatican Council, the *ex sese et non ex consensu ecclesiae*, ("of themselves and not from the consent of the church") and so he goes on to say: "This is not to say that reception by the faithful is in any way constitutive of the infallibility, freedom from error or irreversibility of a dogmatic statement, but that it is necessary for its recognition

---

38. Macquarrie, *Christian Unity and Diversity*, 99.

39. Macquarrie, *On Being a Theologian*, 164. Macquarrie's positive comments on the papacy are mentioned by Miller, *Divine Right*, 125, 127, 133–34.

40. Santer, "Communion, Unity and Primacy," 290.

41. Kasper, *That They May All Be One*, 146.

as such."[42] Needless to say, there are degrees of reception, but without reception authority is virtually meaningless. What would it take to achieve reception, to re-receive the Petrine ministry for Anglicans, and equally what would it mean for Roman Catholics to "re-receive and re-conceive this office and ministry in order that other churches and communities could receive it not as a burden but as a gift?" Santer's splendid response to the question is that such re-reception on the part of both Anglicans (and indeed others in the Reformation traditions) and Roman Catholics would be enabled by "a shared re-reading of history leading to a sharing and purification of memories."[43] This is in fact what Pope John Paul II called for in his encyclical on ecumenism, *Ut Unum Sint* (paragraph 2), and indeed what John Macquarrie has called for when he speaks of the need for "an atmosphere of love and purgation."

Ecumenism

In 1999 Macquarrie wrote about ecumenism in this vein:

> As far as ecumenism is concerned, I was, like many people of my generation, at one time an enthusiast. But in fact, as one looks back over what has happened in the twentieth century, the ecumenical movement seems to have run out of steam. The World Council of Churches, which seemed so important when it was founded in 1948, has been a disappointment. In the first place, it was never entitled to call itself a "world council" for the largest of all the Christian churches and the only one which might be called a worldwide church, namely, the Roman Catholic Church, has never belonged to the WCC. In the second place, in its earlier years the WCC was very deeply under the influence of Barthian theology, which among other things meant that there could be no dialogue with non-Christian religions. Fortunately, that particular phase passed, but it was succeeded by one in which the WCC became intensely political and seemed to be more influenced by ideology than by theology.[44]

This is a rather bleak view of ecumenism and it may be challenged in different ways. For example, while it is true that the Roman Catholic

---

42. Santer, "Communion, Unity and Primacy," 292–93.
43. Ibid., 295.
44. Macquarrie, *On Being a Theologian*, 64.

Church has not belonged to the WCC, that has more to do with its own ecclesiological principles than it has with the WCC as such. Finally, there is a Catholic theological conviction that its membership in the WCC would diminish and even damage its claim that the one church of Christ "subsists" in the Roman Catholic Church.[45] Further, Macquarrie fails to note that since the late 1960s the Roman Catholic Church has been a full participant in the Faith and Order Department of the World Council of Churches, dealing with matters of Christian doctrine and tradition. That is not full participation in the World Council, but it is not nothing!

Providing the foreword to a more recent book entitled *Rome and Canterbury, The Elusive Search for Unity*, Macquarrie gives us a bird's-eye view of his reading of church history since the sixteenth century and of the ecumenical movement: "The Reformation was, to some extent, a revolt against materialism and an attempt to establish the essential spirituality of the church, but it failed and produced in the end only a broken church." He goes on to note the fissiparous dimension of ecclesiology in the Reformation tradition, something that Bishop Newbigin commented on, and then ends the section with these remarkable words: "Then something like a miracle began to manifest itself. The so-called Ecumenical Movement was born. The many relatively small Christian groups began to seek unity among themselves, and *this is possible only in an atmosphere of love and purgation.*" One assumes that he means "love and purgation" not only on the part of the individual and within local congregations, but also at the widest and highest ecclesial levels. The challenge is obvious and Macquarrie entertains no romantic or optimistic view. Rather, he insists that: "There is a very long way to go, and much of it still lies ahead of us. The Protestant bodies will have to find the way to Rome and Rome will have to find an acceptable way of accepting them and whatever may have been valid in the character of each. Overarching these divisions of the West, attention must be given also to the difference between East and West."[46] This is his way of acknowledging that the ecumenical movement is dialectical and complex, and should not be understood in terms of its goal as simply unilateral. Consistently throughout his entire oeuvre Macquarrie insists on a legitimate pluralism in the church, provided that this pluralism does not lead to a basic lack of cohesion. Uniformity is not synonymous with unity. He is,

---

45. See Vatican II's *Lumen Gentium/Constitution on the Church*, paragraph 8.
46. Macquarrie, "Foreword," viii.

therefore, suspicious of a unity that would fail to acknowledge and respect the different Christian ecclesial traditions.

He sees a paradigm of a single Christian communion that combines both unity and pluralism exemplified in his own Anglican Communion. "Anglicans affirm the basic doctrines of Catholic faith, but allow latitude in the interpretation of these doctrines and believe that free but responsible theological discussion rather than appeal to a detailed *magisterium* is the best way of sifting truth from falsity."[47] Admittedly, in the run-up to and in the wake of the 2008 Lambeth Conference, the combination of unity and pluralism working effectively in genuine communion had become acutely problematic for Anglicans. Even acknowledging the present difficulties, however, the way in which Macquarrie understands the issue is still commendable, that is to say, when it comes to truth and falsity it is better not to have immediate recourse to a detailed *magisterium*.

Because of this panoramic vision of a united Christian communion, but not uniform in expression, Macquarrie is utterly opposed to schemes of Christian union, schemes based on national or geographical lines particularly. The various Christian traditions have their own integrity and, "like an art style, cannot be mixed with other traditions without loss of its distinctive appeals."[48] Avery Dulles provides a strong endorsement of Macquarrie's perspective here, and goes on to insist along with Macquarrie that the only really worthwhile unity between the churches is a unity that gathers up all their complementary and enriching diversity.[49] Macquarrie makes the further cogent point that "In the history of religions, syncretism has always proved to be a weakness and there is no reason to suppose that it would be any different in the context of Christian ecumenism." For Macquarrie, one of the most worrying concerns of the ecumenical movement is this failure to recognize the value of the various Christian traditions, and he is quite scathing in his criticism of a certain kind of ecumenist: "There has come into being a kind of ecclesiastical jet set, whose members seem always to be on the point of departing for conferences in Jakarta or Uppsala, or just getting back from other conferences in Accra or Caracas."[50]

Most schemes of union for Macquarrie seem to aim at the greatest degree of compromise and uniformity. The best existing model for Christian

---

47. Macquarrie, *On Being a Theologian*, 119.
48. Macquarrie, *Christian Unity and Diversity*, 17.
49. Dulles, "Ecumenical Strategies for a Pluralistic Age," in his *Resilient Church*, 186.
50. Macquarrie, *Christian Unity and Diversity*, 19.

unity, as he explores it in his 1975 *Christian Unity and Christian Diversity*, is the uniate model, "which we find in the relation of the Roman Catholic Church and the so-called 'Uniate' churches of the East." His concern is not with the way that these unions came about historically, "some of them decidedly shady." The value is in the model itself, which at the same time allows union with Rome, and a measure of autonomy for the individual churches, for example, in the areas of liturgy and canon law. The uniate model thus keeps together both values of unity and legitimate pluralism. Here also veteran ecumenical theologian Avery Dulles finds himself in agreement with Macquarrie, although he points out that uniatism often carries with it the negative sense of submission of one church to the doctrinal and ecclesiological principles of another, thus undermining the enriching complementarity already alluded to.[51]

Macquarrie's position has not been without its critics, most notably the late Lesslie Newbigin, Bishop of the Church of South India, the subject of chapter 2 of this book. Newbigin immediately points out that whether one likes it or not, united churches have proliferated and that "millions of Christians are living in such united churches, daily thanking God for the blessing of unity."[52] Newbigin, as a life-long committed ecumenist, had a much clearer vision of the impact of such church unions than Macquarrie. His own experience in the united Church of South India bears witness to at least the value of that successful experiment in church union. "In 1965, after an absence of eighteen years," writes Bishop Newbigin,

> I returned to Madras as bishop to serve the same churches which I had known two decades earlier as competing congregations. I did not find that they had become uniform: on the contrary I found a rich variety of styles in worship and practice. What I found was congregations less concerned about their own affairs and more ready to think in terms of God's will for the life of the city as a whole, less like competing clubs each trying to enlarge itself and a little more recognizable as sign and foretaste of God's kingdom.[53]

Where church unions function in this way, the problems to which Macquarrie was drawing attention are diminished.

---

51. Dulles, "Ecumenical Strategies for a Pluralistic Age," 188. See also the helpful comments of Geoffrey Wainwright, *Doxology*, 319–22, as well as the ecclesiological comments and glosses found throughout his *Lesslie Newbigin, a Theological Life*.

52. Newbigin, "All in One Place or All of One Sort?" 293.

53. Ibid., 299.

It is also difficult to avoid the conclusion that Macquarrie's antipathy toward pragmatic ecumenical solutions is somewhat colored by the theology of his Glasgow doctoral supervisor, Ian Henderson. Henderson deeply distrusted what he took to be schemes of ecclesial union that neglected in principle the particularities of churches.

> In (Henderson's) *Power Without Glory* the implied criticism of ecumenical theology is greatly developed. Here he makes the point that ecumenical language "is designed not to describe but to conceal" and that it is "a fiesta of double-think." . . . There is a language which conceals in order to evade, a language which does not explore open theological possibilities but rather manipulates the data in order to arrive at predetermined results.[54]

Macquarrie does not share every aspect of Henderson's point of view as is established in his personal and published commitment to ecumenism, but there remains a lingering distrust of pragmatic bureaucracy that can seem to give short shrift to important theological presuppositions and convictions that have contributed to Christian disunity in the first place.

It would be most unfortunate to end this account of Macquarrie's approach to ecumenism on a negative note because that would certainly not be congruent with his perspective. In what must have been his very last published comment on ecumenism he says this: "Impossible, do we say? I don't think so, but it will need enormous patience, for which we should all be praying. The prayer itself produces the way to recovery."[55] That final comment recognizes both the priority of God's grace and initiative as well as hopeful realism, and underscores the absolute need for what has been termed "spiritual ecumenism."

Pride in the Church

Distancing himself from any kind of ecclesial triumphalism, Macquarrie nonetheless believes that there is a right kind of pride in the church, a pride in the church's history or activities. "Such pride becomes sinful and blameworthy only when it settles into a hardened attitude of superiority or when it becomes egocentric and issues in an exclusive and contemptuous attitude

---

54. Macquarrie, "A Modern Scottish Theologian," in his *Thinking About God*, 210–11.
55. Macquarrie, "Foreword," viii.

to others."⁵⁶ Yet again this attitude exemplifies John Macquarrie himself. There is no attitude of superiority in the man, no egocentricity, no contempt of others. His ecclesiology and sacramental theology establish this to a fine degree. He knows that "The church shows, even if only weakly and fitfully, a hidden glory that is striving to find expression and realization," but it does show this glory. In 1970 Macquarrie wrote: "My personal love and admiration for the Roman Catholic Church, and my great commitment to the Catholic form of Christianity are great. . . . I rejoice that even now we are so close to each other, and look forward to our drawing still closer together in the decades ahead."⁵⁷ If this is true of his theology of church and of his ecumenical commitment, it is amply verified in his sacramental theology, and especially his eucharistic theology.⁵⁸ There can be no doubt concerning Macquarrie's commitment to the cause of ecumenical ecclesiology.

56. Macquarrie, *Theology, Church and Ministry*, 107.

57. Macquarrie, "What Still Separates us?" 53.

58. For a comprehensive account of Macquarrie's sacramental theology, see Cummings, *Theology of John Macquarrie*, 231–74.

6

Avery Dulles, SJ, *Models of the Church*

Christians have radically different visions of the Church. They are not agreed about what the Church really is.

AVERY DULLES, SJ.[1]

Dulles's single greatest hit was undoubtedly "Models of the Church," published in 1974, and instantly claimed as a classic.

MARK MASSA, SJ.[2]

Avery Dulles has been described as "surely the greatest Catholic theologian of the English-speaking world of the twentieth century."[3] The two quotations that open this chapter provide an excellent introduction to the American Jesuit theologian Avery Dulles, whose contributions to ecclesiology have been outstanding. This is most especially true, as Mark Massa points out, in respect of Dulles's *Models of the Church*. Massa says that it has been claimed as a classic. He is right, because since its first publication in 1974 it has continued to be used in Catholic courses on ecclesiology

1. Dulles, *Models of the Church*, 7.
2. Massa, "A Model Theologian," 12.
3. Nichols, *Engaging Theologians*, 157.

and, indeed, well beyond the Catholic Church. The book's success is largely based on Dulles's acknowledgment that Christians have radically different visions of the church, and yet if ecumenism is to be taken seriously, there must be some way in which to bring together the giftedness of all ecclesial communities and churches in the development of ecclesiology.

The Church is Mystery

It is important to begin with the acknowledgment that the church is mystery. God is mystery and the church is about the work of God in the world, and so the church participates in the mystery that God is. This is certainly the fundamental starting point of Vatican II's Constitution on the Church. Vatican II rejected an initial schema on the church in which the first chapter was called "The Nature of the Church Militant." The first chapter in the finally accepted Constitution on the Church, by way of contrast, is "The Mystery of the Church." This way of understanding and this form of expression find an echo in the thinking of Pope Paul VI: "The Church is a mystery. It is a reality imbued with the hidden presence of God. It lies, therefore, within the very nature of the Church to be always open to new and ever greater exploration."[4] The church is mystery because its core reality is God, and God is mystery. Dulles writes: "In some respects we shall in the end have to accept a reverent silence about the Church, or for that matter about any theological reality. But we should not fall into the negative phase prematurely, until we have exhausted the possibilities of the positive."[5] Given the fundamental reality of the church as mystery, what ecclesiology needs to do is to maintain "a kind of mental juggling act, we have to keep several models in the air at once."[6]

Images and Models of the Church

After the Constitution on the Church introduces the fundamental idea of the church as mystery, the document then proceeds in paragraphs 6–7 to illuminate something of the mystery with a plethora of images from Holy Scripture. Almost contemporary with Vatican II's Constitution on the

---

4. Dulles, *Models of the Church*, 10.
5. Ibid., 10–11.
6. Ibid., 2.

Church is the Yale New Testament scholar Paul Minear's 1960 outstanding book, *Images of the Church in the New Testament*. Informed by the Constitution's many images for the church and influenced by Paul Minear's book, Dulles proceeds to explore further ecclesiological images. As he did so, he recognizes not simply the multiplicity of images of the church, but also something not less important: "The psychology of images is exceedingly subtle and complex. . . . They speak to man existentially and find an echo in the inarticulate depths of his psyche. Such images communicate through their evocative power."[7] He does not go on to develop this psychological point at any great length, but the very fact that he makes it at all indicates at least an incipient awareness that the appeal of images, and might we say also of doctrines, has something to do with the human psyche and in respect of both individual and ecclesial tradition the pre-history of the psyche. Different images, different doctrines, have their appeal at more than the intellectual or conceptual level.

"When an image is employed reflectively and critically to deepen one's theoretical understanding of a reality it becomes what is today called 'a model.'"[8] What he means by a model is more or less equivalent to analogy, but analogy free of the subtleties of neo-scholastic philosophy and theology. Models or analogies become centrally important, maintains Dulles, because "the method of models is applicable to the whole of theology, and not simply ecclesiology."[9] Dulles is not the only theologian to use the method of models in ecclesiology. The Benedictine theologian Jerome P. Theisen sets out nine models, and Richard P. McBrien, a foremost American Catholic ecclesiologist, provides three models.[10] The use of models in theology, and not only in ecclesiology, may "prevent us from making concepts and symbols into idols. It helps us realize that the infinite can never be captured in the finite structures of language."[11] The question is inevitable: is it possible to verify the value of models in theology, the value of models in ecclesiology? Dulles provides a refreshingly pragmatic and persuasive answer: A model is valuable if it leads to "an intensification of faith, hope and charity, or to an increase of what St. Paul calls the fruits of the Holy

---

7. Ibid., 12.

8. Ibid., 15. For useful comment on as well as critique of Dulles, see Fuellenbach, *Church*, 108–66.

9. Dulles, *Models of the Church*, 4.

10. Theisen, *Ultimate Church*; McBrien, *Catholicism*, 710–14.

11. Fuellenbach, *Church*, 109.

Spirit: love, joy, peace, patience, kindness, and the like (cf. Gal. 5:22–25)....
We assess models and theories, therefore, by living out the consequences to which they point."[12] Perhaps we may put it like this—ecclesiological orthodoxy necessarily goes hand-in-hand with moral and spiritual orthopraxis.

Historical Perspective

One of Avery Dulles's great theological strengths, evidenced throughout his entire theological corpus, is a highly developed historical awareness. In ecclesiology this leads him to state: "From 1600–1940 the juridical or societal model was in peaceful possession, but it was then displaced by that of the Mystical Body, which has been subsequently dislodged by three other models in rapid succession: those of the People of God, Sacrament, and Servant."[13] This very brief historical survey, then, becomes the springboard for his development of six basic models of the church, reflecting theology and ecclesiology from 1974–2002. In the first edition of his book he said, "From the writings of a number of modern ecclesiologists, both Protestant and Catholic, I have sifted out five major approaches...."[14] These models are the church as:

1. Institution.

2. Mystical Communion.

3. Sacrament.

4. Herald.

5. Servant.

With the advent of Pope John Paul II and one of his favorite images of the church, "Community of Disciples," Dulles went on to add this as model six. Mark Massa recognizes Dulles's nuanced historical sensitivity especially when it comes to his six models of the church.

> What Dulles had found in his mastery of the history of Catholic theology was that the tradition had always, wisely, allowed various theological emphases to flourish.... The *real* Catholic past was far more diverse, pluralistic and messy than many in the twentieth century church understood or wanted to believe. Those who

12. Ibid., 19.
13. Ibid., 22.
14. Ibid., 1.

sought to force that broad tradition into any single model—but especially into the institutional model—were betraying the tradition, not restoring it.[15]

Dulles's first model is the church as institution. To get at the heart of this he makes two critical points. First, demonstrating his historical awareness, he insists that "In spite of the overemphasis on the institutional in official Roman Catholic theology, especially since the Reformation, the institutional model of the Church has rarely been advocated in its purity."[16] There was undoubtedly in the wake of the sixteenth-century Reformations a certain hardening or institutionalizing of Catholic ecclesiology in response to the Reformers' critiques and protests. In Dulles's historical analysis the patristic period and the Middle Ages up to about the thirteenth century was "relatively free of institutionalism." The emergence of institutionalism after the reformations and the polemics of the sixteenth century reached its high point with Pope Pius IX and the growth of ultramontanism climaxing in Vatican I in 1869–70. Even while some echoes may be found in Vatican II's Constitution on the Church, perhaps inevitably, the Constitution is for the most part free of institutionalism and juridicism.

Nonetheless, Dulles is surely right to maintain that

> Institutionalism . . . is not the same thing as the acceptance of the institutional element in the Church. . . . By institutionalism we mean a system in which the institutional element is treated as primary. . . . Institutionalism is a deformation of the true nature of the Church, a deformation that has unfortunately affected the Church at certain periods of its history, and one that remains in every age a real danger to the institutional Church.[17]

Any human society to be effective for any purpose whatsoever must have some kind of institutional arrangements: offices, officers, rules and regulations, etc. To think otherwise seems very unreal. But this necessary kind of institutional apparatus is entirely different from an excessive emphasis on it that seems to make the institutional apparatus self-serving rather than serving and attending to others. English theologian Nicholas Lash is of the same mind when he says, "It has long seemed to me that demands for a 'non-institutional Christianity' are not so much theologically defective

---

15. Massa, "A Model Theologian," 15–16.
16. Dulles, *Models of the Church*, 38.
17. Ibid., 27.

as sociologically naïve."[18] The church as institution must continue. Some of the most obvious consequences of institutionalism are clericalism, juridicism, and triumphalism. As a post-graduate student in the Faculty of Divinity in the University of Glasgow in the late 1970s, I recall having a conversation with Professor Ernest Best, a well-known Presbyterian New Testament scholar, in which he insisted that the institutionalism in the local presbyteries of Northern Ireland and Scotland was not less intense than what I observed in the Catholic Church. Institutionalism is perhaps a recurrent temptation in any ecclesial tradition.

The second model is the church as mystical communion. "The concept of the Church as a communion harmonizes with two biblical images that have figured prominently in modern Catholic ecclesiology, the Body of Christ and the People of God."[19] This particular model of communion has gained increasing acceptance as a way of understanding the church not only in Catholicism, but throughout the Christian world. Communion ecclesiology, or the church as mystical communion, puts the stress on interpersonal relationship, both with the triune God (before the Father, in Christ as his Body, through his Spirit), and with the members themselves, rather than on describing the church in terms of an institution of salvation or a perfect society.

The Catholic systematic theologian Dennis Doyle points out that there is no one version of communion ecclesiology, more or less corresponding to Dulles's second model. "Communion ecclesiology represents an attempt to move beyond the merely juridical and institutional understandings by emphasizing the mystical, sacramental, and historical dimensions of the church. It focuses on relationships, whether among the persons of the Trinity, among human beings and God, among the members of the communion of saints, among members of a parish, or among the bishops dispersed throughout the world."[20] In the light of this description it is possible to recognize the vertical dimension of communion ecclesiology, that is to say communion with God, and the horizontal dimension, communion with others. Doyle provides six different but related accounts of communion ecclesiology, but accounts that are better described as related rather than in competition. First, a Congregation for the Doctrine of the Faith version,

---

18. Lash, *Voices of Authority*, 19.
19. Dulles, *Models of the Church*, 42, slightly adapted.
20. Doyle, *Communion Ecclesiology*, 13.

which is notable for its emphasis on the priority of the church universal and the importance of certain visible church structures.

> The concept of communion, which appears with a certain prominence in the texts of the Second Vatican Council, is very suitable for expressing the core of the Mystery of the Church, and can certainly be a key for the renewal of Catholic theology. . . . However, some approaches to ecclesiology suffer from a clearly inadequate awareness of the Church as a *mystery of communion*, especially insofar as they have not sufficiently integrated the concept of *communion* with the concept of *People of God* and of the *Body of Christ*, and have not given due importance to the relationship between the Church as *communion* and the Church as *sacrament*.[21]

Second, a Rahnerian version, and as one would expect in reflection influenced by Karl Rahner, characterized by an emphasis on the sacramentality of the world and on the communion with God that exists within all of humankind. Third is a fashion in line with theology of Hans Urs von Balthasar, with an emphasis on the uniqueness of Christian revelation and on its aesthetic character. Fourth comes a version of communion ecclesiology shaped by liberation theology. As one would expect, this version underscores the option for the poor and the political implications of communion. Fifth is what Doyle terms a contextual version, in which the emphasis is on gender, ethnicity, and social location as the context for appreciating relationality, very contemporary ecclesiological preoccupations. Finally, the sixth version is a reforming version. This model of communion ecclesiology emphasizes the need for Roman Catholics to challenge radically their own ecclesiological presuppositions in the interest of ecumenical progress. As Doyle insists, the six versions of communion ecclesiology, arguably a teasing out of what Dulles means by "mystical communion," are not isolated and watertight categories. The concepts and language flow in and out of the six versions even as Doyle's broad characterization remains in place. Even though the actual term "communion" does not feature largely in the documents of Vatican II, this has become the preferred umbrella term under which to find the essential lineaments of what it means to be church. The model of the church as communion also has a broader appeal across the Christian traditions. It is articulated by the World Council of Church is as follows:

21. Ibid., 1–22.

> The notion of *koinonia* (communion) has become fundamental for revitalizing a common understanding of the nature of the church and its visible unity.... The term is being reclaimed today in the ecumenical movement as a key to understanding the nature and purpose of the church. Due to its richness of meaning, it is also a convenient notion for assessing the degree of communion in various forms already achieved among Christians within the ecumenical movement.[22]

The value of this model of communion suggests strongly that it has a privileged place in ecclesiology, even if it may not be regarded exclusively as *the* model of the church.

The third model of the church for Avery Dulles is the church as sacrament. In the years prior to Vatican II, the notion of the church as sacrament, a strongly patristic theme, began to be explored again. Examples of theologians writing in this vein prior to Vatican II would be Henri de Lubac, SJ, Edward Schillebeeckx, OP, and Otto Semmelroth. Some words of de Lubac provide a good summary of what Dulles means by this model, and in fact he cites his fellow Jesuit in this regard. "If Christ is the sacrament of God, the Church is for us the sacrament of Christ; she represents him, in the full and ancient meaning of that term, she really makes him present. She not only carries on his work, but she is his very continuation, in a sense far more real than that in which it can be said that any human institution is its founder's continuation."[23] This sacramental way of thinking about church is found quite explicitly in a number of texts from Vatican II, to take a couple of examples. "By her relationship with Christ, the Church is a kind of sacrament or sign of intimate union with God, and of the unity of all humankind"—from the Constitution on the Church, paragraph 1. "Rising from the dead, he sent his life-giving Spirit upon his disciples and through this Spirit has established his Body, the Church, as the universal sacrament of salvation"—from the Constitution on the Church, paragraph 48. Dulles himself provides a nice summary understanding of the church as sacrament in these words:

> The Church understands God as the loving Father of all men; it celebrates and preaches God's redemptive love extended to all. The Church therefore takes it for granted that others besides

---

22. World Council of Churches, *Nature and Purpose of the Church.*

23. de Lubac, *Catholicism,* 29. See also his *Splendor of the Church;* and Schillebeeckx, *Christ the Sacrament;* and Semmelroth, *Church and Sacrament.*

Christians are recipients of God's grace in Christ. The Church is the place where it appears most clearly that the love that reconciles men to God and to one another is a participation in what God communicates most fully in Christ.[24]

Dulles's fourth model is the church as herald, a model that powerfully resonates with the emphasis on the Word God in the Reformation traditions. "This model is kerygmatic, for it looks upon the Church as a herald—one who receives an official message with the commission to pass it on.... For the Church to be a place in which the word of God is truly heard, it is necessary that the word should never be imprisoned or bracketed by the Church."[25] Another fundamental text from Vatican II, the Constitution on Divine Revelation, provides the foundations for this ecclesiological self-understanding. "The Church has always venerated the divine Scriptures as she venerated the Body of the Lord," paragraph 21. A fine commentary—and what this means in practice—may be found in some words of Carlo Martini, SJ, a biblical scholar and former Archbishop of Milan:

> The Word nourishes the believer, who listens to it in humility and obedience; it encourages, consoles, comforts and illuminates just as the sacramental Body of Christ nourishes, encourages, consoles and comforts.... The Eucharistic Body of Christ which is made present in our altars is inseparable from the Scriptures: the Eucharist is effected through words which are found in the Scriptures; it is explained during the liturgy, again with words from the Scriptures; it is situated in the saving plan as revealed and described in the Scriptures. Scriptures, the historical Christ, the Eucharistic Christ—these are three strictly related realities and it would be heresy to separate them or to claim to understand them in isolation.[26]

On a practical note, this is surely an ecclesiological model that has been taken to heart among many Catholics throughout the world. In almost every Catholic parish today one will find Bible study groups, Scripture sharing groups, and in the catechesis provided for the Rite of the Christian Initiation of Adults in which Scripture plays a major role—all these are ways of verifying the emergence of the church as herald in the hearts of ordinary congregations.

24. Dulles, *Models of the Church*, 63.
25. Ibid., 68–69.
26. Martini, *Reflections on the Church*, 38.

To appreciate something of Dulles's fifth model, the church as servant, it would be helpful to contrast ways of thinking about the church in the nineteenth and twentieth centuries. While it is something of a caricature, it also captures something of the truth to see the church of the nineteenth and twentieth centuries as a secure fortress defending its members against a hostile world. For Dulles this contrasts strongly with Pope John XXIII and Vatican II as "registering a dramatic change of attitude," an attitude not only marked by a greater degree of openness to the world but also by a sense of service to the world. This sense of connection with service to the world finds expression particularly in Vatican II's Pastoral Constitution on the Church in the Modern World, described by Dulles in these words: "The Pastoral Constitution on the Church in the Modern World, the most novel and distinctive contribution of Vatican II, outlines a completely new understanding of the relationship between the Church and the world of our day."[27] In the Constitution itself we read: "[The church] acknowledges the legitimate autonomy of human culture and especially of the sciences" (paragraph 59);

> This Sacred Synod proclaims the highest destiny of man and champions the godlike seed that has been sown in him. It offers to mankind the honest assistance of the Church in fostering that brotherhood of all men which corresponds to this destiny of theirs. Inspired by no earthly ambition, the Church seeks but a solitary goal: to carry forward the work of Christ himself under the lead of the befriending Spirit. And Christ entered this world to give witness to the truth, to rescue and not to sit in judgment, to serve and not to be served (paragraphs 3, 92).

Finally, we come to the sixth model of Dulles, reflecting the theology of Pope John Paul II in his encyclical *Redemptor Hominis* (paragraph 21), "The Church is the community of disciples." The actual term "Community of Disciples" is not found in the documents of Vatican II, but apparently on over twenty occasions those documents refer to church members as "disciples." In terms of his own personal reflections, Dulles says "While admitting certain complexities in this question (Did Jesus found the church?), I would contend that the central difficulty is solved once one recognizes that Jesus did deliberately form and train a band of disciples, to whom he gave a share of his teaching and healing ministry. 'Community of Disciples'

---

27. Dulles, *Models of the Church*, 83.

is precisely what Jesus undoubtedly did found."[28] The ecclesiologist John Fuellenbach invites us to consider this model in the light of Mark 3:3–15, which he summarizes as "called, to be with, and to be sent out." He believes that the church as a community of disciples finds its emphasis on the second of these three aspects, "to be with." "To be a disciple means first and foremost to be with the Lord, to have been called by him into intimacy, to have firsthand knowledge of him."[29] These sentiments bring to fuller expression Dulles's meaning.

Conclusions

Towards the beginning of *Models of the Church*, Dulles writes:

> The method of models or types, I believe, can have great value in helping people to get beyond the limitations of their own particular outlook, and to enter into fruitful conversation with others having a fundamentally different mentality. Such conversation is essential if ecumenism is to get beyond its present impasses. Also, as Catholics have discovered since Vatican II, the problem of internal dialogue within a single denomination is almost equally acute.[30]

This statement is of enormous importance. Not only do his carefully articulated ecclesiological models reach across ecumenical divisions towards concord and harmony, but they also fulfill this function within the Catholic Church itself. Since the close of Vatican II in 1965, the last half-century or so has witnessed a growing polarization in the Catholic Church, perhaps most especially in the American Catholic Church. Dulles's argument here is that his ecumenical approach of models in ecclesiology may also help Catholics within their own church to get beyond the impasse of their own ecclesiological visions and divisions. Ecclesiologist Joseph Komonchak helps to elucidate this valuable insight: "His hope was that by tracing differences in practice or in theory back to guiding images and controlling models of the church, Catholics would learn to be at once more modest and self-critical about their own positions and more respectful of the views of others because they would appreciate the inability of any single vision

---

28. Dulles, *A Church To Believe In*, 8.
29. Fuellenbach, *Church*, 114.
30. Dulles, *Models of the Church*, 5.

of the church to exhaust the riches of its mystery."[31] This is clearly an area where Dulles's earlier comment about the psychology of images comes very fruitfully into play. In other words, difference is not necessarily divisiveness. "Certain types of persons will be drawn to certain models."[32]

He offers some practical conclusions to his models methodology. First, practice tolerance and accept pluralism, within limits, in respect of models of the church. "We must recognize that our own favorite paradigms, however excellent, do not solve all questions. Much harm is done by imperialistically seeking to impose some one model as the definitive one."[33] Second, recognize the weaknesses of ecclesiological models. "Each model of the Church has its weaknesses; no one should be canonized as the measure of all the rest. . . . [They are] mutually complementary. They should be made to interpenetrate and mutually qualify one another."[34] Third, recognize that some ways of thinking are to be rejected. "Although all the models have their merits, they are not of equal worth, and some presentations of some models must positively be rejected."[35] Notice the balance in this statement, that is to say, "*some* presentations of some models" are to be rejected. In putting it this way, Dulles recognizes our all too human capacity for exaggerated emphasis, for getting things out of perspective, and neglecting other points of view. As one theologian has put it, "There is no model to end all models."[36]

---

31. Komonchak, "Many Models, One Church," 12.
32. Dulles, *Models of the Church*, 184.
33. Ibid., 24.
34. Ibid., 25.
35. Ibid.
36. Fuellenbach, *Church*, 110.

7

Frances M. Young on Theology, Mary, and Prayer

Faith is never hereditary; there are no second-generation Christians. We all know this, but we also know that family and environment contribute a lot to the accent with which we speak our Christian language.

ROWAN WILLIAMS[1]

Introducing Frances Young

These opening words from former Archbishop of Canterbury Rowan Williams are self-evidently true, and they also offer an excellent segue to introducing Frances Young and her contribution to ecumenical ecclesiology. Frances M. Young (born 1939) is a New Testament and patristic scholar, but has a wide range of interests in systematic and ecumenical theology also. She is an ordained Methodist minister. Both of her grandparents were Methodist ministers and her own parents were Methodist local preachers. With a background in the classical languages, Greek and Latin, her doctoral work was in patristics and so "her theology is therefore rooted in the early classics of Christian thought but has been through modernity without

1. Williams, "Profile: Frances Young," 1.

being contained by it."[2] Rowan Williams describes her approach to theology in these terms:

> Frances has a natural "pitch" in her theological voice which owes a great deal to that fundamentally traditional but entirely unfussy and rather undogmatic orthodoxy that typifies so much of Methodism; a "feel" for essentials that does not get too worked up about tightly confessional matters or formulae but revels in the task of communicating in word and image a sensed abundance.[3]

Unlike many other academics, Frances Young remained as a teacher of theology at the University of Birmingham in England all of her life. Rowan Williams comments: "Her commitment to an academic institution has been parallel in character to her commitment to the Church—without illusion and with patience. There are no academic utopias any more than there are ecclesial ones, or human utopias overall."[4] Although Frances Young has not published an ecclesiology as such, her entire Christian pilgrimage as well as for many publications touch centrally on the reality of what it means to be church.

Vocation to the Methodist Ministry

Describing ministerial vocation in the church Frances Young says, "If you speak of vocation rather than career, the overtones are those of dedication rather than ambition."[5] In ordinary terms, her career in theology in the academy has been eminently successful. In many ways, however, her academic work in theology has spilled over into dedicated service as a Methodist minister. In her case it may indeed be preferable to think of her years in academic theology as much a vocation as her Methodist ministry.

She is insistent on the priority of God's call in the making of a minister. "Ministry begins there, and the distinctive thing about it lies there."[6] The fundamental characteristic of vocation in the Holy Scriptures has to do with this priority of God's call. This is evidenced especially in the prophet Jeremiah (1:4–6) and it is likely, she believes, that Jeremiah's experience and

---

2. Ford, "Wilderness Wisdom," 160.
3. Williams, "Profile: Frances Young," 1.
4. Ibid., 5.
5. Young, "The Implications of Vocation," in Young and Wilson, *Focus on God*, 3.
6. Ibid., 4.

meditation influenced St. Paul. Reflecting on the notion of vocation in the Pauline literature, for example, his Damascus Road experience as well as Galatians 1:11–13, 15; Romans 8–9; 2 Corinthians 2:15–16, and also on the treatment of vocation in the systematic theologian Karl Barth, she acknowledges readily that every believer has a vocation, a vocation that stems from being a member of Christ's holy body. At the same time, there is the equal acknowledgment of the specific vocation of the minister or the ordained within this more general baptismal vocation. "Paul's own call and commissioning," she avers, "is distinct from that of his converts."[7] Distinct, yes, as he discerns God's call to him to do a particular something in a particular ministry; separate, no, in the sense that this doing is grounded in his being as a member of Christ's body. The minister is someone who represents in an outward and visible way, and in various modes, the fundamental reality of God and of God's love. That is what makes the minister a representative person. There is something quite extraordinary in God's call: "How odd of God to choose the Jews, or Paul, or me!"[8] She finds this theology of vocation well expressed in the Methodist Covenant-service:

> I am no longer my own, but thine. Put me to what thou wilt, rank me with whom thou wilt; put me to doing, put me to suffering; let me be employed for thee or laid aside for thee, exalted for thee or brought low for thee; let me be full, let me be empty; let me have all things, let me have nothing; I freely and heartily yield all things to thy pleasure and disposal.[9]

She does not shirk the difficult question, "How is one to trust or to know the authenticity of the divine call as distinct from a figment of one's imagination?" The answer that she offers, and perhaps ultimately the only satisfying experiential answer that can be given, is "by their fruits, you shall know them." There is therefore in the experience and the following out of a divine call or vocation a certain risk. "There is a risk—there is a risk in the commitment of Christian faith and in responding to God's vocation, and the validity of the vocation is only discovered in its outworking, its fruits."[10]

---

7. Ibid., 7.
8. Ibid., 11.
9. Ibid.
10. Ibid., 13.

Frances M. Young on Theology, Mary, and Prayer

The Nature of Theology

In his description of Frances Young's theology, Rowan Williams writes as follows: "What matters isn't system, if that implies a complete vision viewable at arm's length, but persuasion and invitation into the normally fractured and stumbling speech of believers transformed by the awareness of God alongside in pain and unclarity."[11] It seems to me a very appropriate description of theology for any Christian theologian. It is particularly appropriate for Frances Young, whose commitment to the discipline is best described in her own words: "For me there never can be any gulf between theology and spirituality, the intellectual quest and the pilgrimage of discipleship."[12]

One of the most noticeable and indeed notable things about Frances Young's theology is her willingness and ability to cross over the normal boundaries and genres of theological writing. "Paradoxically, perhaps, the readiness to cross conventional academic boundaries, not only between different bits of theology (patristics, New Testament exegesis, systematics) but between what many would consider respectable and non-respectable genres for an academic, is not an ignoring of limits and boundaries but a recognition that certain styles of academic discourse need to be cured of their aspirations to self-sufficiency."[13] Indeed, her willingness and ability to close these traditional academic boundaries in theology have given her what Rowan Williams calls "the pastoral edge," and he goes on further in his description to say: "As much as any of the patristic theologians she discusses, she is always writing 'applied theology'; and the care, patience, reticence and subtlety of her work remind us that 'applied theology' is emphatically not less complex and demanding an exercise than systematic construction."[14]

An ordained minister must live in and out of the Holy Scriptures. That is one of the great emphases and the discoveries of the Reformation, and a ministerial consequence of Avery Dulles's model of the church as herald. It is captured superbly by the late sixteenth- and early seventeenth-century Anglican priest-poet George Herbert. In his practical manual for priestly living, *A Priest to the Temple,* Herbert commends as centrally important

---

11. Williams, "Profile: Frances Young," 7.
12. Young, *Can These Dry Bones Live?* xi.
13. Williams, "Profile: Frances Young," 3.
14. Ibid., 4.

the place of Holy Scripture. "The country parson is full of all knowledge. . . . But the chief and top of his knowledge consists in the book of books, the storehouse and magazine of life and comfort, the Holy Scriptures. There he sucks and lives."[15] If Herbert has captured the importance of Holy Scripture for a minister, Young knows all about this. Thinking of the past in terms of biblical literacy she writes, "The way that people understood their own lives was once shaped by patterns and models found in Scripture, and conversely, people read their own lives into Scripture."[16] No less than our forebears, authentic Christian faith invites us to be absorbed into the world of the scriptural texts. She is not advancing an uncritical approach to Scripture by any means, but rather an approach that serves to deepen our growing awareness of God-in Christ-through the Spirit-in the Scriptures. She draws an analogy when she says,

> It is not, I suggest, all that different from what happens when we read novels or go to the theater. Empathy means we come away with our consciousness in some sense transformed. . . . There has to be interaction between text and reader; there are multiple potential meanings, because the Bible speaks in many different ways, many different languages, to people in many different places, cultures, situations, or dilemmas.[17]

Frances Young also emphasizes the importance of tradition. "The minister mediates the wider tradition to the local group, which would otherwise be in danger of becoming ingrown, insular and even deviant."[18] She does not come at this issue of tradition from an epistemological or hermeneutical viewpoint, but rather, she comes at it from what one might call a common sense theological position.

Everyone is aware nowadays that what might have been at one time a particular ministerial responsibility is now exercised and discharged by others, for example, counseling, social work, and so forth. Is there, then, in these times anything particularly distinctive about the pastoral care exercised by the ordained in the church? There is no doubt in her mind that

---

15. Tobin, ed., *George Herbert*, 204. Young knows Herbert's wonderful poem on preaching, "The Window." See her *Can These Dry Bones Live?* 1–2.

16. Young, *Brokenness and Blessing*, 12.

17. Ibid., 23–24. These ideas are drawn out at much greater length in her fine book, *The Art of Performance*.

18. Young, "Using the Tradition as a Theological Resource," Young and Wilson, *Focus on God*, 33.

there is something distinctive about the ministerial care of the ordained and it is this: "A ministry grounded in God will be primarily concerned with fostering a sense of God's reality in the midst of the whole of life and celebrating it. . . . But celebrating the reality and being of God embraces everything, and this will only happen as people's minds and imaginations are fired by God, his love, his beauty, his presence." For a minister of the church to foster this sense of God's sheer wonderful and beautiful reality, the minister must be steeped and saturated in the broadest sense in the theological tradition of the church.

> To effect this demands of the minister that he be a theological resource person at the local level, knowing and communicating the treasures of the faith passed down over many generations, fostering reflection and questioning in the search for ways of discerning God in the present, giving people the bread of life not only at the communion rail, but through the word of preaching, the faithful teaching—not indeed acting as an authority, but as one who like Socrates may be a "midwife" stimulating the minds of others to think thoughts they had no idea they were capable of. In other words, a minister has a maieutic educational role.[19]

Notice in her description here a balanced emphasis on both word and sacrament—the minister is in his teaching and preaching role breaking open the Word of God, and he is offering the bread of life at the communion rail. Scripture and Eucharist make the church. What is eminently clear from all of her writing is the importance of so-called academic theology for pastoral ministry:

> There is a mood abroad in society which elevates activity at the expense of thought and disciplined study, which devalues pure research in favor of applied, which turns the word "academic" into a word of criticism, a synonym for irrelevant, impractical or niggling. People are prepared to accept slipshod thinking and superficial slogans, as long as some practical contribution is the outcome. And this mood has invaded the church.[20]

Young believes that there are various reasons for this lack of interest in past theological controversies. First, there is the widespread devaluing of the past in modern culture. Emphasis tends to be on the present, and moreover, on the scientific and technological aspects of progress. The past

---

19. Ibid., 14.
20. Young, *Can These Dry Bones Live?* 2.

and especially past theological controversies seem to moderns of little or no importance. Second, in pluralist, tolerant, and ecumenically minded modern societies, there is a fear that past controversies ignite once again the polemical flame. This is not the case because she firmly believes that difference is not the same thing as divisiveness. Third, in both contemporary society and in the church there is a primacy given to personal experience and practical experience over studying past thinkers or past controversies, or, indeed, reaching out to people today who think differently. There needs to be, she believes, a getting to know others in depth and this depth is achieved fundamentally by reading—about their lives, their history, and their convictions and beliefs.[21] This primacy given to personal and practical experience has become much exacerbated through extensive and global use of the Internet—blogging, tweeting, etc. No one would denounce the importance of these technological breakthroughs, but though Young does not say so in so many words, there can be no substitute for personal reading and study, or face-to-face encounter with a person or a text, or, for that matter, other non-verbal expressions of the tradition, and thus avoiding the contemporary temptation of becoming a technological solipsist. This is how she put it: "Why should we suppose that because twentieth-century technology is superior, twentieth-century grasp of Christianity is always superior?"[22]

The lifelong apprenticeship to those who have been in the grip of Christian sensibility in the history of the tradition is not only intellectual, though it is all of that, but it is also prayerful, mystical, and contemplative. If he is to initiate others into the mystery of God's gracious presence, then the awareness of that presence must be for the priest or minister something habitual and deeply textured into his own life. "The minister needs to be plugged into the tradition and to be able to use it creatively to nurture fresh thinking about the meaning of Christian faith today."[23]

When this lifelong apprenticeship, this exciting apprenticeship to the entirety of the Christian tradition does not take place, and the priest or minister of the church, or indeed anyone who has responsible for the religious education of the young, many people become disenchanted thinking that they must entertain an infantile view of Christian matters. "The church

---

21. Young, "Using the Tradition as a Theological Resource," Young and Wilson, *Focus on God*, 35.

22. Ibid., 36.

23. Ibid., 33.

is in danger of becoming a sect of the credulous, simply because we do not value the proper childish activities of investigating what most interests us with boldness and enthusiasm."[24] People have the need, even if they do not always feel the need, for a more in-depth appreciation of the Christian reality. If this is not mediated to them by clergy, by preachers and teachers in appropriate ways, then the abandonment of the church and its tradition begins to make some sense to them. They have grown out of an unreflective understanding, and are searching for something more. If they do not find that something more that is fundamentally satisfying, even exciting, then they may well go somewhere else, judging the church and its tradition to be irrelevant. Priests and ministers of the church need to prepare themselves as rigorously as possible so that they may proclaim the message generated by the Scriptures and the tradition as attractively and persuasively as possible. They need to appreciate, with Frances Young, that

> academic study at its best is not retreating to an ivory tower, but learning to submit oneself to discipline, to the objectivity of a text, to the reality of other people's thoughts, to high standards of honesty and attention to detail, to a special kind of humility, to an ability to listen across the centuries and across cultural divergences for the accents of truth mediated through a diversity of forms.[25]

Mary

Much progress has been made since Vatican II on ecumenical dialogue and agreement concerning the blessed Virgin Mary. One thinks, for example, of the Lutheran-Catholic dialogue of 1992, and of the Anglican-Catholic dialogue (the Seattle Statement) of 2005.[26] As well as these formal dialogues, of course, there has been an abundance of writing about Mary from different ecumenical perspectives. Writing in 1992, Frances Young says "[Since 1982], my own explorations have led me in the unexpected direction of the Virgin Mary."[27] Her appreciation of Mary, Mother of Jesus, is something that has grown over the years. One could argue that there has been

---

24. Young, *Can These Dry Bones Live?* 12.

25. Ibid., 16.

26. See Anderson et al., *The One Mediator, the Saints, and Mary*; Bolan and Cameron, *Mary, Grace and Open Christ*.

27. Young, *Can These Dry Bones Live?* x.

for Young a mutually critical correlation, to use David Tracy's theological methodology,[28] between her own lived experience and the theological tradition of the church. In terms of her own lived experience, suffice it to say that growing up both in England and in Northern Ireland in the 1950s would not have been the most auspicious context for the development of Marian appreciation. Hostility and polemics between Protestants and Catholics especially in Northern Ireland meant that there was little appreciation, and certainly no devotion, to Mary. This is what she writes in terms of growing up concerning Mary: "Like most Protestants I had given little thought to Mary except at Christmas, and had grown up hearing the occasional Freudian remark about Marian devotion being natural for a celibate priesthood."[29] When it comes to the theological tradition, in the course of her patristic studies, especially of Cyril of Alexandria, her Marian horizon broadened. It was the mutually critical correlation between her own patristic studies on Mary and her own lived experience that brought her to a greater depth of appreciation of Mary.

At Easter 1991, Young went on a pilgrimage to Lourdes in France at the invitation of Jean Vanier, the founder of the L'Arche communities.[30] She says of that occasion, "I accepted Jean's invitation with many misgivings—I feared Lourdes would raise all my liberal Protestant hackles." What she found, however, was that "the place was about purification, not so much miraculous cures as deeper levels of healing and acceptance. Traffic gave way to wheelchairs, and the strong received ministry from the weak."[31] On the same occasion she was the preacher at an Anglican Eucharist in the upper Basilica at the shrine, and later on she attended the celebration of the Roman Catholic Eucharist for those pilgrims coming from English speaking countries. She writes, "the services were virtually identical."[32] The similarity between the services would not have been much of a surprise to Frances Young. What is far more interesting is what happened to her as a result. "In that context I found myself traveling through the Passion with Mary, and preaching at her feet on Easter morning at the Anglican Eucharist in the

---

28. Tracy, *Blessed Rage for Order*, 32–34.
29. Young, "Theotokos," 341.
30. See Young, ed., *Encounter with Mystery*.
31. Young, "Theotokos," 351.
32. Young, "Great Thanksgiving Prayer," 80.

Upper Basilica. That Easter it became profoundly important to me that she was the vehicle of purification and blessing through her Son."[33]

In respect of this growing appreciation of and devotion to Mary one of Young's lifelong theological friends, David Ford, has written: "Perhaps the most sensitive yet fruitful question is about [Frances's] relationship with Mary the mother of Jesus. One phenomenon over the years as Arthur's mother is her growing identification with Mary.... [It] is not quite so usual among Methodists."[34] We have seen something of this growing identification, but a word of explanation is in order. Arthur is one of Frances Young's sons, physically and mentally handicapped since birth. With her husband she has looked after her son, in the midst of a demanding pastoral and academic career. As Ford intimates, Young's growing devotion to Mary is associated with this experience with her son. Here is a poem that she has written that gives us a profound sense of her growing identification with Mary:

> Mary, my child's lovely.
> Is yours lovely too?
> Little hands, little feet.
> Curly hair, smiles sweet.
>
> Mary, my child's broken.
> Is yours broken too?
> Crushed by affliction,
> Hurt by rejection,
> Disfigured, stricken,
> Silent submission.
>
> Mary, my heart's bursting.
> Is yours bursting too?
> Bursting with labor, travail and pain.
> Bursting with agony, ecstasy, gain.
> Bursting with sympathy, anger, compassion.
> Bursting with praising Love's transfiguration.
>
> Mary my heart's joyful.

33. Young, "Theotokos," 351.
34. Ford, "Wilderness Wisdom," 158.

Is yours joyful too?"

One of the features of Marian reflection that has become particularly meaningful to Frances Young is the notion of Mary as the type of the church, something echoed in the last chapter of Vatican II's Constitution on the Church that is given over to a consideration of Mary.

> Mary, in her community and receptivity, enabled the birth of Christ into the world. And what does the Magnificat mean? It means that the humble are lifted up. It is characteristic of the rich and the powerful to be in control, and the temptation of the do-gooder is to be in control. That is not the way of the Magnificat. The Magnificat requires humility and waiting upon God. This waiting leads to worship.[35]

Prayer

"Praying is both the simplest and the hardest part of the theological task. Without it theology is barren."[36] It is a temptation for one who is immersed in the excitement of studying theology, of teaching theology, to think that this important analysis and critique is all that needs to be done. Young is insisting, and rightly, that without the commitment of prayer, this approach to theology yields little fruit. Awareness of God and response to God puts everything in perspective: "In God's presence all the questions just fade away, as you realize the immensity of the infinite, divine reality with which you are confronted."[37]

What has been said above is true for every Christian, and especially for those engaged in the study and teaching of theology. But it is even more pressing for one in ministerial service to the church. "The minister's task is to nurture and facilitate discernment of God, response to him, and the positive shouldering of responsibility in his world."[38] This approach refuses any kind of dualism or separation between relationship with God/response to him and relationship with creation/responsibility in his world. Both must go together. An exclusive emphasis on the former creates a sense of unreality so that the world and all that goes on in it seems to be of little

---

35. Young, "Great Thanksgiving Prayer," 89.
36. Young, "Addressing God," in Young and Wilson, *Focus on God*, 106.
37. Young, *Brokenness and Blessing*, 47.
38. Young, "Addressing God," in Young and Wilson, *Focus on God*, 105.

importance. Attending to the things of the world without relationship with God reduces Christianity to a socio-political phenomenon and eclipses any sense of transcendence. Young recognizes that the task of the minister as she describes it is shared by the whole Christian community, but the minister's leadership role in this regard prevents the church "from getting ingrown and insular." She offers some very challenging thoughts about the centrality and importance of prayer, not only for the church's minister, but perhaps especially for him or her: "It is [the minister's] job to foster the church's theological self-awareness, and prevent it stagnating."[39] At the center of this responsibility lies the public prayer that is worship. This is all important.

> God is not simply one to be talked about, but one to talk to and listen to. . . . Praying should provide an ever-broadening perspective which is less and less self-concerned and more and more confident, trusting and God-centered, thus providing the sure ground which produces the fruit of loyalty and faithfulness against the odds. It should thus deepen theological awareness, and that awareness should preclude the kind of faith which melts away at the first difficulty. . . . [W]ithout critical thinking [prayer] easily becomes idolatry. Without the input of knowledge outside ourselves, it rapidly becomes narcissistic—an emotional self-indulgence or even self-delusion.[40]

One can see here that a commitment to theology, public worship and personal prayer are interwoven and necessarily go together. Prayer cannot be dissociated from thinking.

> Should we not give God respect enough to think before and as we pray? Without constantly expanding thought, prayer tends to become a conventional routine following familiar tram-lines. Without mental concentration, it sinks into a meaningless ritual, vain repetitions. Without critical reflection, it easily becomes idolatry. Without the input of knowledge outside of ourselves, it rapidly becomes narcissistic, or as she says, "an emotional self-indulgence or even self-delusion."[41]

---

39. Ibid., 106.
40. Ibid., 106–10.
41. Ibid., 108–9.

Young is not opposed to conventional prayer routines, and equally she is not opposed to spontaneity in prayer, but she is very insistent that "praying and thinking belong together."[42]

She has wise things to say about the prayer of petition, recognizing, of course, that prayer is also adoration, thanksgiving, and contrition. "It might transform our prayer if it were seen not as a way of petitioning for revelation or help, but as entering into a relationship in which part of the responsibility for decision-making rests with us, and that together with God we are involved in creating the future, both individually, and as a community."[43] Simple, but very helpful words. There is nothing manipulative nor magical nor superstitious about petitionary prayer. It never has to do with bargaining with God. Rather, it is textured into the very fabric of life, with all its ups and downs. This is how Young describes it:

> Prayer has been described as being attuned to glory and pain, the agony and ecstasy of the universe; and in the Jewish and Christian tradition, prayer is in fact, above all, a corporate commemoration, the bringing to mind, or recollection, of a sacred history which draws the worshiper into a community and a narrative that both gives identity and which the individual into perspective, eliciting a response of praise, thanksgiving, repentance, and obedience or renewal.[44]

It would be difficult to improve on this comprehensive description of prayer.

Conclusion

Ecclesiology is done in different ways and not simply through formal courses. Summarizing and synthesizing Frances Young's theological reflections on theology, Mary, and prayer is an indirect way of doing ecclesiology. It is precisely through her reflections on these subjects that her ecclesial horizon has become more decidedly ecumenical. She remains a devout and committed Methodist minister, but with a significantly developed ecumenical outlook.

---

42. Ibid., 109.
43. Ibid., 108.
44. Young, "Dare We Mention Prayer?" in his *Dare We Speak of God in Public?* 139.

8

Eucharist, Ecumenism, and George Hunsinger

I like it when the Liturgy of the Sacrament and the Liturgy of the Word are celebrated in the worship service every week, if not more.

GEORGE HUNSINGER.[1]

Introducing George Hunsinger

George Hunsinger is an ordained Presbyterian minister and systematic theologian. He is at present the Hazel Thompson McCord Professor of Systematic Theology at Princeton Theological Seminary in New Jersey. Having received his BD from Harvard University Divinity School, he went on to do a PhD at Yale University. His published work over the years has focused primarily on the theology of Karl Barth, and Hunsinger is one of the premier Barth scholars in the United States. That Barthian interest has brought him into association with what has been called post-liberal theology, a Yale "school" of theology characterized by theologians like George Lindbeck (born 1923) and Hans Frei (1922–88).

---

1. Hunsinger, *Eucharist and Ecumenism*, 332.

The Eucharist and Ecumenism

Hunsinger has developed a keen interest in ecumenical theology, and in 2008 he published a book with Cambridge University Press that has attracted considerable interest entitled *The Eucharist and Ecumenism: Let Us Keep the Feast*. Hunsinger emphasizes that the book is primarily addressed to members of his own Reformed tradition. "I have tried to show the Reformed how they could adopt some previously contested views—on the historic threefold offices (bishop, presbyter, deacon), on Eucharistic sacrifice, and on the consecrated gifts—without theological compromise."[2] His proposals are meant to help the Reformed move towards visible unity. As he puts it with great passion, "The most urgent ecumenical goal cannot be self-preservation, to say nothing of ecclesiastical self-aggrandizement. The most urgent goal, as elusive as it is, must be to achieve substantive convergence so that wider Eucharistic sharing can begin."[3] It is one of the greatest tragic ironies of the Christian tradition that the very rite that should hold all Christians together in the deepest bonds of communion both with the triune God and with each other, that is to say the Eucharist, has been the cause of such enormous divisions, not least stemming from the sad chapters of the sixteenth century. Hunsinger recognizes that the cause of Christian unity can be about ecclesial self-preservation. That would simply be a form of ecclesial narcissism which has no place in the following of Jesus who came "not to be served but to serve" (Mark 10:45), and who prayed that his followers "may be one even as we are one (Jesus with the Father), I in them and thou in me, that they may become perfectly one, so that the world may know that thou hast sent me and hast loved them even as thou hast loved me" (John 17:22–25). Anglican theologian Mark McIntosh has written of Hunsinger's book that "it is a work marked by a deeply considered insightfulness, by genuine ingenuity, and, throughout, by a gracious aspiration to understand the very best in each position being examined."[4]

What Is Ecumenical Theology?

Right at the start of the book Hunsinger insists that ecumenical theology is different from what he calls "enclave theology" and "academic theology."

2. Ibid., 274.
3. Ibid.
4. McIntosh, "Christ the Word Who Makes Us," 255.

Enclave theology is "a theology based narrowly in a single tradition that seeks not to learn from other traditions and to enrich them, but instead to topple and defeat them, or at least to withstand them. . . . It is not really interested in dialogue but in rectitude and hegemony. . . . Enclave theology makes itself look good, at least in its own eyes, by making others look bad."[5] He acknowledges that no church or ecclesial tradition is entirely free or immune from the temptation of enclave theology, or more popularly and pejoratively "dogmatism." There is a constant temptation to learn one's theology *against* someone else. Certain way of doing theology is to say the least ecumenically sterile and barren. At the same time, Hunsinger believes that academic theology, at least in the liberal mold of theology that characterizes so many western institutes of higher education, is marked by "its lack of allegiance to established confessional norms."[6] Although he does not quite put it like this, academic theology in Hunsinger's construal does not care about the church and its tradition. Rather, it insists upon its own open-ended, critical-liberal project without any need to recognize or to respond to ecclesial allegiance. No one arguably would contest the importance of the critical element in theology. It liberates from horizons that are too narrow, it liberates from enclave theology. Yet, Christian theology is parasitic upon the Christian community with its long history of reflection, with the Holy Scriptures and with the Holy Table of the Eucharist, with its creeds and liturgies, with its doctrinal formulations and ethical concerns. Critical reflection in academic departments of theology should also be marked by a passion for construction, for building up the church, so that the world may believe. At the same time, one could say that academic theology has often saved the churches from fundamentalism and authoritarianism in theology. While he appreciates this contribution, perhaps Hunsinger would say that this kind of academic theology wants to reflect on the Christian tradition but without "belonging." Belonging is all-important for him in view of the overriding goal of Christian re-union.

For the most part, Hunsinger is addressing his own Reformed tradition, attempting to show "how the Reformed tradition might be brought closer to Roman Catholic and Eastern Orthodox features without compromising Reformed essentials."[7] It seems to me, however, that Hunsinger's address pertains also to the Roman Catholic tradition. There must be

5. Hunsinger, *Eucharist and Ecumenism*, 274.
6. Ibid., 2.
7. Ibid., 11.

equally an attempt to show how the Roman Catholic tradition might be brought closer to the Reformed tradition, without compromising Catholic essentials.

Real Presence

Hunsinger quotes Lutheran theologian and ecumenist George Lindbeck as follows: "The Eucharist tastes bitter in a divided church."[8] Hunsinger wants to get beyond division. Thus, careful attention is given to Aquinas, Luther, Calvin, and Vermigli, all giants within their own traditions, but he concludes that a patristic understanding of eucharistic real presence might well be possible for Protestant churches today. In the first millennium of Christianity's existence, there was no fragmentation of the church on the scale of that which took place in the sixteenth century. Looking back to that millennium for a eucharistic medicinal compound that will heal this broken body of the church can only be a good thing.

The patristic understanding to which Hunsinger refers is "transelementation." Relying on the work of Orthodox theologians Alexander Schmemann (and to a lesser extent John Zizioulas) "transelementation," in Greek *metastoicheia*, is understood as Christ joining the bread to his life-giving flesh so that the two become one.[9] Hunsinger shows throughout the book that transelementation as a category for thinking about the Eucharist reflects elements of Reformed teaching, is central to Orthodox theology of the Eucharist, and is omnipresent in the patristic period. "As one can imagine, this is of huge strategic significance, for if Rome finds the Eucharistic teaching of the Orthodox acceptable, and if something very like this might be recoverable among the Reformed . . . then a fruitful and necessary meeting point might well be rediscovered."[10] The late Orthodox theologian John Meyendorff puts it like this: "(Orthodox theologians) would consider a term like 'transubstantiation' . . . improper to designate the Eucharistic mystery, and generally use . . . such dynamic terms as 'transelementation' (*metastoicheiosis*) or 're-ordination' (*metarrhythmisis*)." And so for Hunsinger, while transubstantiation asserts one substance being changed into another, transelementation asserts that "one object is suffused with

---

8. Ibid., 22.
9. Ibid., 63.
10. McIntosh, "Christ the Word Who Makes Us," 256.

another's reality and power."[11] Although Hunsinger acknowledges repeatedly that what he means by transelementation is not exactly the same transubstantiation, he maintains the hope that the two might live in "a kind of peaceful coexistence."[12] Perhaps one might say that transelementation flows from a more platonic metaphysics while transubstantiation, especially in its Thomist form, is closer to Aristotelian metaphysics. Whether this be the case or not, it is certainly the case that there is no revealed metaphysics. Furthermore, Hunsinger's basis for his hope for transelementation is that Orthodox affirmations of transelementation have not posed a real problem for Catholic recognition of the Orthodox Eucharist. If Reformed Christians might be able to identify with transelementation, then this might move Reformed and Catholics closer together on this divisive issue of the Eucharist.

The late Canadian Catholic ecumenical theologian, Margaret O'Gara, has some very good things to say about Hunsinger's contribution. She rightly notes that the sixteenth-century Catholic Council of Trent acknowledged that the reality of Christ's eucharistic presence was so great a mystery that it could hardly be expressed in words, and further, though transubstantiation was "most apt" to express something of the mystery, it did not intend to present transubstantiation "as the only acceptable conceptual framework."[13] O'Gara further underscores what she understands to be the real importance of transubstantiation: "In both cases (Aquinas and the Council of Trent), the idea of transubstantiation was intended to counter materialist understandings and materialist Eucharistic practices, as well as to affirm the mysterious but real conversion of the elements of bread and wine into the body and blood of Christ."[14] The council fathers at Trent, in using the term transubstantiation, were using basically the term for eucharistic presence that they knew. They were not endorsing any particular philosophical application or analysis of it. Perhaps, then, transubstantiation does not need to be the great impediment to eucharistic insight and agreement that it so often seems.

Of course, Hunsinger recognizes that continuing difficulties remain, for example, using the consecrated/transelemented elements for any purpose other than communion. He wishes to avoid eucharistic adoration outside the celebration of the Eucharist, a traditionally very difficult issue

11. Hunsinger, *Eucharist and Ecumenism*, 74.
12. Ibid., 78.
13. O'Gara, "Toward the Day," 263.
14. Ibid.

for Reformed Christians. At the same time, he goes so far as to say the following:

> Transelementation would allow the very idea of "Eucharistic duration" to extend beyond the celebration of the sacrament. In the Word and by the Spirit, the sacramental union once accomplished would persist, because Christ by his Spirit would have joined himself to the elements for Eucharistic purposes of communion. In the reserved sacrament the union would not be static but would continue to be living and operative albeit in a quiescent state. It would be "at rest," so to speak. It would persist without becoming crudely lifeless or "thing-like." It would represent Christ's enduring commitment to attest and impart himself by means of the consecrated elements.[15]

This is a hugely interesting statement. The language does not immediately echo the linguistic tradition of Catholic eucharistic adoration, true enough, but it is not all that far removed from it. If Christ has committed himself to be "there" in the eucharistic elements for his people, if he really imparts himself by means of these consecrated elements, I find it difficult to see how a Catholic could take major issue with Hunsinger's understanding. Hunsinger continues: "In short, why should the sacramental union once instituted not continue—not only *in usu*, but also *extra usum*, though still *pro usum*?"[16] That last clause in the sentence is entirely Catholic theologically. Now, obviously, all of this hangs on the notion of "transelementation." Undoubtedly, that will continue to be debated in the scholarly community. But it seems a most generous point of view. That generosity continues as Hunsinger concludes: "Since few non-Catholics are likely to embrace the doctrine of transubstantiation, an alternative that is not unacceptable to Roman Catholicism is greatly to be desired. It would seem that transelementation could be embraced by a wide variety of non-Catholics."[17]

Eucharistic Sacrifice

Hunsinger's opening paragraph on the topic of eucharistic sacrifice is a splendid synthesis of the Reformation protest:

---

15. Hunsinger, *Eucharist and Ecumenism*, 84.
16. Ibid., 87.
17. Ibid., 91.

> Nothing was denounced more vehemently by the Reformation than the Roman Catholic view of the Mass as a "propitiatory sacrifice." To the Reformers almost everything wrong with Catholicism seemed to coalesce at this point. The Catholic Mass combines several distinct abuses. They were mercenary, because Masses for the dead were shamelessly bought and sold. They were ecclesiological, because the priesthood had usurped an illicit role at the expense of Christ's people. Above all, they were soteriological, because the Roman Church had arrogated powers to itself that did not belong to it, but only to Christ. Zwingli, Luther, Calvin were relentless, in the grand sixteenth-century style, in exposing these interlocking evils.[18]

He goes on to note that as a result of ecumenical dialogue and sacramental/liturgical development, Reformation concerns about eucharistic sacrifice no longer seem so problematic. As with the issue of eucharistic presence, he pays careful attention to the points of view of the classical Reformers, Luther, Zwingli, and Calvin. All three were convinced that Christ alone is our salvation in and through his all-sufficient sacrificial death. All three were equally convinced that the Roman Mass attempted to repeat this unrepeatable and unique sacrifice of Christ. "It thereby made God's grace conditional rather than gratuitous."[19]

Hunsinger then examines on the Catholic side Aquinas and the Council of Trent. He reaches towards the following conclusion after his sensitive explorations and expositions of both sides of the ecumenical divide:

> The sacrifice of Calvary is unrepeatable; and second, the Eucharist is not a meritorious work. In turn, the proposal developed here has been, first, that the unrepeatable sacrifice becomes sacramentally present, in the power of the Holy Spirit, as a memorial; and second, that the meritorious work of the Eucharist belongs entirely to the agency of Christ while not excluding a role of active participation, again in the power of the Holy Spirit, for the church, in pleading Christ's eternal sacrifice.[20]

Hunsinger is no romantic ecumenical theologian. He recognizes, along with the Methodist ecumenical theologian Geoffrey Wainwright for example, that eucharistic sacrifice is probably the area of greatest difficulty in the field of eucharistic theology for classical Protestants. While there is

18. Ibid., 95.
19. Ibid., 110.
20. Ibid., 181.

no room for optimism, there is room for hope that just as with the doctrine of eucharistic presence so too with eucharistic sacrifice there has been movement closer one to another through both ecumenical dialogue and sacramental/liturgical development.

Eucharistic Ministry: Controversies

"Yet even if difficulties could be resolved at the conceptual level, entrenched habits of mind would still remain. As long as Zwingli remains our liturgical master, it will be hard for us in the Reformed tradition to benefit from the ecumenical progress occurring elsewhere." Moving on from eucharistic presence and sacrifice he realizes just how perplexing the issues surrounding eucharistic ministry are. "Throughout the ecumenical movement, it has become increasingly, and even painfully, clear that without significant agreement about Eucharistic ministry, the unity that we seek will elude us."[21]

Vatican II's "Decree on Ecumenism" helps to sharpen the issues: "[We] believe that especially because of the lack (*defectus*) of the sacrament of orders . . . [the ecclesial communities] have not preserved the genuine and total reality of the Eucharistic mystery" (paragraph 22). There is a severe way of understanding these words. That severe way would amount to something like this: "Since Protestant churches have a defective ministry with a defective sacrament, they are not really churches at all, but merely 'ecclesial communities.'"[22] This is a very widespread view among Roman Catholics. However, Hunsinger points out, using the Catholic theologians Jared Wicks, SJ, and Cardinal Walter Kasper, that there is a less severe approach to this issue. Wicks understands the term *defectus* to mean "flaw" and not "absence." This is a most important distinction. "Flaw" means imperfection, logically, therefore, something less than perfect or complete. "Absence," on the other hand, defines the situation where someone or something is not present. It is a more totalizing term than flaw. Jared Wicks writes: "Using sacramental terminology, the *res tantum* is given whole and entire, namely, union with Christ, life in the Spirit, and access to the Father."[23] The Latin tag *res tantum* means receiving the grace that is given by the sacrament, that is to say, communion with the triune God. In other words, "a defective means

---

21. Ibid., 190.
22. Ibid., 191.
23. Wicks, "'Ecclesial Communities' of the Reformation," 10–13.

of grace can still deliver the whole *res tantum* of salvation."[24] There may be an imperfection or a flaw from the Catholic perspective of sacramental theology, but it is not simply a matter of the sheer absence of grace. Cardinal Walter Kasper writes in a similar vein:

> Only in the sacramental and institutional respect can the Council find a lack (*defectus*) in the churches and ecclesial communities of the Reformation. Both Catholic fullness and the *defectus* of the others are therefore sacramental and institutional, and not existential or even moral in nature; they are on the level of the signs and instruments of grace, not on the level of the *res*, the grace of salvation itself.[25]

Putting these points of view of both Wicks and Kasper together Hunsinger concludes: "On this somewhat more generous note, *defectus* seems to imply that while, for ecclesial communities, Christ may be mediated under a sacramentally defective form, he is nonetheless present in a truly saving way."[26]

He takes up the question, "Who has the authority to ordain?" and recognizes that this takes us to the controverted issue of apostolic succession.

> In the Roman Catholic Church, apostolic succession means episcopal succession. Only the bishop has the authority to ordain, because only the bishop stands in the unbroken line of ordination, conferred by the laying on of hands, that stretches all the way back to those whom the apostles themselves first ordained. While Catholic theology recognizes that the first ordinands were not bishops in the diocesan sense that later became normative, it holds that the diocesan bishop emerged as their successors. The Catholic Church also recognizes that apostolic succession must be evangelical as well as episcopal, since bishops are particularly responsible for teaching the apostolic faith. In the Reformed tradition apostolic succession means substantive evangelical succession, but not necessarily episcopal succession. Apostolic succession ordinarily devolves on the presbytery, a regional council of presbyters, not on the bishop. It is therefore the presbytery that has the authority to ordain.[27]

---

24. Hunsinger, *Eucharist and Ecumenism*, 192.
25. Kasper, "Present Situation and Future of the Ecumenical Movement," 11–20.
26. Hunsinger, *Eucharist and Ecumenism*, 194.
27. Ibid., 198–99.

He suggests that both Catholic and Reformed theologians and traditions need to be less severe on this question of the validity of ordination. Often Roman Catholic thinking about ordination is judged to be ontological, while Reformed thinking about ordination is judged to be functional. Hunsinger is unhappy with this admittedly crude distinction:

> Catholics and Reformed would both agree that ordained ministers stand over against the faithful community as well as within it. They would both agree that this being set apart occurs so that essential functions can be carried out for the good of all. They would also agree that anyone set apart by ordination receives the special charism needed for the office to be fulfilled. If the nature of ordination is such that there is no charism apart from a function, and no function that does not require being set apart within the community, then it would seem that ontological and functional elements are so closely intertwined as almost to be inextricable.[28]

This is a very persuasive way of thinking. When it comes to the question of the indelible sacramental character conferred in ordination, Hunsinger seeks for a more dynamic rather than a static understanding. The indelible character might be seen

> more nearly as a gift than as a simple possession, or better, a something possessed only as it is given. . . . And once received, is it not expected to be received ever anew? Is not the charism constantly renewed in the context of ministry, worship, and daily prayer? Is it not actualized again and again in the liturgy through proclaiming the Word, celebrating the Eucharist, and announcing the forgiveness of sins? The charism of ordination would be seen as an irrevocable gift that stands under the promise of continual renewal. It would be seen within a larger christocentric context of active participation and ongoing reception. It would not be a static possession, but would be marked by the lively relations of giving and receiving in equipment for ministry.[29]

It would be difficult to find a more attractive way of representing what has been understood traditionally by the "indelible character."

Next, Hunsinger turns his attention to the question of episcopate in the Reformed traditions. This is what he writes:

---

28. Ibid., 203–4.
29. Ibid., 204.

> Nevertheless, it seems fair to suggest that for the sake of ecumenical unity and rectification, the Reformed churches would do well conscientiously to embrace the threefold pattern of ministry as indicated by BEM (the Lima Statement). The Reformed will not only need to overcome a historic aversion to hierarchy and the episcopate. They will also need to accept a central role for the Bishop of Rome, along conciliar lines. . . . Visible unity cannot be said to have been well-maintained in churches lacking the historic episcopate. . . . Without alignment into the historic episcopate, there would seem to be little hope of an ecumenical future. . . . If the Reformed are to take the imperative for visible unity seriously, they must struggle at this point, as all churches must struggle at some point, with the need for their own ecclesial conversion. They must find a way to stretch, without theological compromise, into the need for ordination by bishops who themselves have been ordained in the historic succession of bishops.[30]

This is a very generous recognition on Hunsinger's part. He is proposing that the Reformed tradition not only finds room for the episcopate but also for the episcopacy of the Bishop of Rome. Although much work and growing still need to be done undoubtedly, just this recognition gives great ecumenical grounds for hope. It is in line, of course, with the kind of thinking proposed by Pope John Paul II in his 1995 encyclical on ecumenism, *Ut Unum Sint*, "That They May Be One," in which he requested the Christian traditions of the world and their theologians to reflect on ways in which the Petrine ministry could be shaped so as to benefit all traditions. The Pope asked that other traditions help him "to find a way of exercising the primacy which, while in no way renouncing what is essential to its mission, is nonetheless open to a new situation" (paragraph 95). That is, at least in part, what Hunsinger is doing here, responding positively to this papal invitation. The Pope continued in that text:

> Could not the real but imperfect communion existing between us persuade Church leaders and their theologians to engage with me in a patient and fraternal dialogue on this subject, a dialogue in which, leaving useless controversies behind, we could listen to one another, keeping before us only the will of Christ for his Church and allowing ourselves to be deeply moved by his plea "that they may all be one . . . so that the world may believe that you have sent me" (John 17:21) (paragraph 96).

---

30. Ibid., 207–11.

Theological Imaginations

Hunsinger thinks it is helpful to contrast three different types of theological imagination. The first type is the Roman Catholic type:

> The Roman Catholic imagination is a sacramental imagination. Representation and mediation are the categories it associates with the sacraments. These categories emphasized the unity between Christ and the church. When they are not balanced by categories of witness, however, the church is tempted to identify itself, its institutions, and its hierarchy with the presence of Christ. The dangers here are the dangers of triumphalism and sacralization. These dangers arguably attend the Catholic understanding of Eucharist and ministry.[31]

The second type is the Reformed imagination:

> The Reformed imagination, by contrast, is a verbal imagination. Witness and teaching are the categories it associates with God's Word. These categories serve to bring out the distinction between Christ and the church. When they are not balanced by categories of sacramentality, however, the church is tempted to separate itself, its congregations, its presbyters and its presbyteries, from the presence of Christ. The dangers here are the dangers of intellectualism and secularization. These dangers arguably attend the Reformed understanding of Eucharistic and ministry.[32]

These two forms of the Christian imagination bear more than a family resemblance to the distinction developed by David Tracy in his *The Analogical Imagination*, the analogical imagination and the dialectical imagination. The former is more characteristic of Roman Catholicism and Eastern Orthodoxy, the latter of the Reformed traditions.[33] Hunsinger, however, points to a third type of theological imagination which he calls the Chalcedonian imagination:

> This type can appreciate the sacramentality of the Word and the witnessing function of the Eucharist, because it sees the activity of the living Christ in his self-witness, self-mediation, and self-anticipation as involving both Word and Sacrament alike in the power of the Holy Spirit. The ministry of the entire church, and of

---

31. Ibid., 218.
32. Ibid., 218–19.
33. See Tracy, *Analogical Imagination*.

> the ordained ministry within it, are given a share, in various degrees and ways, in the one ministry of Christ himself to the world. In this ministry Christ is related to the church, and the church to him, through an ordered pattern of active participation. Between Christ and the church there subsists a unity, a distinction, and an asymmetry in which Christ is always present as the Head of his ecclesial body. Ministry takes place within a christocentric ecclesiology of participation.[34]

The Chalcedonian imagination, one might say, is a creative fusion of the Catholic imagination and the Reformed imagination within a traditional Christological focus. It is replete with ecumenical promise.

Hunsinger's rule of thumb is this:

> Whereas Orthodox views do not always agree with Roman Catholic views, but whereas the Vatican sees no obstacles from its side that would prevent Eucharistic sharing with the Orthodox, it follows that Protestants could achieve a greater degree of ecumenical convergence if they adopted views similar to the Orthodox at those points where they are unlikely to embrace Roman teachings (e.g., "transubstantiation").[35]

Eucharistic Ministry: An Impending Impasse?

Hunsinger poses a number of questions "of ecumenical admonition" to churches with high sacramental traditions: Roman Catholic and Eastern Orthodox. "At every point [these questions] enter a plea for developing less rigid, more differentiated, and more reasonable judgments 'in order that we may all be one.'"[36] Many questions are posed, but I believe that the governing question that seems to direct them all is this:

> If Eastern Orthodoxy and Roman Catholicism need each other in fundamental respects, in order to attain and recover a once and future doctrinal fullness, does that not also relativize any imperious suppositions, insofar as they may exist, that Protestant and other traditions have nothing indispensable to bring the *oikumene*

---

34. Hunsinger, *Eucharist and Ecumenism*, 219.
35. Ibid., 274.
36. Ibid., 220.

with respect to attaining a higher degree of doctrinal fullness in the common apostolic succession?[37]

Having moved through pages of very probing questions he concludes as follows:

> To sum up, the point of this exercise in ecumenical admonition has not been to make any one tradition look good by making others look bad. It has only been to suggest that there are more than enough warts (*defectus*) to go around. No existing church can reasonably claim to be free of them in non-trivial respects. It is perhaps the special vocation of Reformational churches, formed as they are by the greater liberating doctrine of *simul iustus et peccator*, to press the point.[38]

He picks up the question of women's ordination, something that Roman Catholic and Eastern Orthodox maintain that they could never accept, and something now present in many Protestant denominations and he notes that "The ecumenical movement threatens to founder on the shoals of this *impasse*."[39] Hunsinger clearly indicates what all can in a sense see: "The stakes are high but the course is set. It makes no sense for the Roman Catholic Church to pretend that women's ordination in the Protestant churches, including the ordination of women bishops, can be reversed."[40] That is sheer pragmatic realism. For the Protestant churches, as well as those of the Anglican Communion, quite simply there is no going back. The ordination of women is here to stay. This remains a very serious obstacle for the Catholic tradition, both Eastern and Western. It is impossible to predict the future of ecumenism. It is not impossible to pray and to hope for resolution on this difficult issue, even if at this time such resolution looks very shadowy indeed.

Eucharist and Social Ethics

The final section of Hunsinger's book is devoted to "Eucharist and Social Ethics," and has two chapters: "The Eucharistic Transformation of Culture," and "Nicene Christianity, the Eucharist, and Peace." Connections

37. Ibid., 221.
38. Ibid., 231.
39. Ibid., 232.
40. Ibid., 242.

between the Eucharist and social justice have often been made in Catholic eucharistic theology over the past thirty years. Little needs to be said about this particular issue other than what might be called a summons to action. Hunsinger pays particular attention to the connection between social ethics on the Eucharist in 1 Corinthians 11, and also to such ethicists as John Howard Yoder. Some of his final words in this section of the book are particularly worthy of repetition: "The Eucharist as celebrated by forgiven sinners is a living reminder of what can only be attested in humility and hope with respect to cultural transformation. In a difficult world, it is a gift of grace. But grace without the corresponding action is not grace."[41] No one could disagree with those sentiments.

Over against any kind of reductionist Christology or soteriology, or any non-Trinitarian view of God, Hunsinger takes a firm stand with the councils of Nicaea and Chalcedon. Using a phrase of one of his teachers at Yale, the late Hans W. Frei, the importance of Nicaea and Chalcedon lies in their being "conceptual re-descriptions of the [Gospel] narratives." In other words, there is real continuity in Christology and Trinitarian theology from the New Testament through these councils, and that continuity is best described as "Nicene Christianity." In talking about Nicene Christianity, Hunsinger affirms that

> Nicene Christianity begins and ends in worship. Nicene worship is always Eucharistic, directly or indirectly, even as it is always also baptismal and charismatic. These three liturgical elements—baptism, Eucharist, and proclamation—are inseparable from one another. Just as the Word grounds baptism and the Eucharist, so also they in turn symbolize and mediate the Word.[42]

Central to what he calls this Nicene appreciation of the Eucharist is the conviction that "enemy-love stands at the heart of the gospel, at the heart of the Eucharist, and therefore at the heart of mission," and in this regard he cites the Greek Orthodox theologian Metropolitan John Zizioulas: "Of all the forms of love the most significant from the viewpoint of both the Eucharist and of the last times is love for our enemies."[43] And so Hunsinger concludes:

---

41. Ibid., 278.
42. Ibid., 282.
43. Ibid.

Understood in this way, the Eucharist serves as a kind of liturgical bridge, mediating between proclamation and mission. It liturgically enacts the gospel of reconciliation while communicating an ethos of peace to the church, and through the church to the world. The ethos of enemy-love and forgiveness as eucharistically embodied and mediated functions not only vertically but also horizontally; not only individually but also communally; not only in worship but also in witness. The ethos imparted by the Eucharist to mission is an ethos of reconciliation and peace.[44]

Conclusion: Let Us Keep the Feast

Ecumenical convergence does not seem possible without affirming Nicene Christianity, a high view of the Eucharist, and some sort of Episcopal polity. . . . An attempt has been made . . . to keep the Reformed in alignment with the Eastern Orthodox on those points where they cannot follow the Roman Catholics, and where, as far as the Catholics are concerned, the Orthodox view does not seem to be church-dividing.[45]

Realism and a life-giving hope characterized George Hunsinger's ecumenical theology.

At the same time, Hunsinger ends his book with some sad words. "

What I like least, I'm afraid, is the usual form of celebration in American Protestant churches like my own. What does it symbolize when little trays of pre-cut white bread are passed through the pews, to be followed by larger, more cumbersome trays with grape-juice-filled little cups (these days, more often than not, even disposable plastic cups). I feel embarrassed when these services are visited by ecumenical friends. How can they help musing that what is being symbolized here is the essence of Protestant individualism and privatized religion, the alone communing with the Alone (as Plotinus said), a deracinated form of community, giving new meaning to Rahner's phrase "anonymous Christians"?[46]

George Hunsinger's book is generally quite accessible to the informed theological reader. It certainly deserves to be studied carefully by Catholics.

44. Hunsinger, *Eucharist and Ecumenism*, 283.
45. Ibid., 314.
46. Ibid., 332.

Eucharist, Ecumenism, and George Hunsinger

Fr. Ernest Falardeau, SSS, the ecumenical theologian has written recently apropos of the ecumenical import of St. Paul's words in 1 Corinthians 11:

> The most challenging word that Paul gives the Corinthians is that their celebration of the Eucharist is a scandal. The reason, simply put, is because they "do not recognize the body" (1 Corinthians 11:29). Most exegesis of this text stresses the need for holiness in approaching the Eucharist. Yet a deeper consideration of the context of what Paul says in 1 Corinthians 10 and 11 shows that the very purpose of the Eucharist is to deepen the Christian communion (*koinonia*) with God in Christ through the Eucharist. This insight is not Orthodox or Catholic, Protestant or Pentecostal. It is simply what Paul is talking about at the beginning of the Epistle (chapter 1) as well as in chapter 12, where Paul describes the church as the body of Christ and speaks of the interdependence of each member.[47]

Hunsinger helps us in the most profound way to plumb the depths of the Pauline insight concerning our eucharistic interdependence. Hunsinger challenges us ecumenically to respond energetically and now.

---

47. Falardeau, "Eucharistic Challenge," 198.

Conclusion

The Church of God on earth is visibly divided, but in its depth it is graced by the indivisible gift of God. Christians are unfaithful; God is faithful.

Jean M. R. Tillard, OP.[1]

Our series of ecclesial-ecumenical snapshots is now over. I do not say "complete," because in the most profound sense every committed Christian, most especially those who have roles of leadership in the church, constitute ongoing snapshots. "Between nearly all the main historical churches, doctrinal consensus is growing."[2] This is certainly true at the level of global, national, or regional leadership in the Christian churches. One suspects, however, that it may not be quite so true at the local level, at the local churches, parishes, centers where Christians gather to worship Sunday after Sunday. At this level all too often there is a lack of both information and formation in ecumenical matters.

"Committed Christians are shaped by their 'confessional' ethos, and they have to know why some issues are no longer considered divisive."[3] The ways in which we think about ecumenism, the ways in which we speak about other Christians, too often betray an insufficiently informed perspective. While professional theologians constantly engage works in theology flowing from the pens of Christians in other traditions, it is too seldom the case at the local level of leadership. Local clergy, lay Christian leadership in

---

1. Tillard, "*Ex Tenebris Lux*," 199.
2. Ibid., 191.
3. Ibid., 192.

Conclusion

local churches and parishes have responsibility for many tasks. One of those tasks must be the ongoing study of theology, a study that reflects some of the remarks of Frances Young in the chapter devoted to her. Progress at the local ecumenical level, with ordinary people in the pews, cannot go ahead unless the leadership blazes the trail and encourages it.

Would it not be a marvelous thing, for example, for a Christian community to read John Wesley's *Letter to a Roman Catholic* during the week of prayer for Christian unity? What a fine commitment it would be during Lent, when Christians tend to have a more seriously devout approach to their lives, for a Catholic parish to have weekly presentations that consider the various chapters of the Decree on Ecumenism? The work of Avery Dulles, SJ on models of the church could offer a firm basis for adult theological study. I could imagine that the ecumenical development of Frances Young in respect of Mary would be a suitable theme for engaging Catholics, and indeed not only Catholics, during the month of May, traditionally given over to reflections on and devotion to Mary. One could go on and on with these suggestions. Suffice it to say that it is important for us all to develop a passion for church unity and if that passion is to maintain its energy throughout the course of our lives and in our local Christian communities, that energy needs to be fed. It is the hope of this author that this little book may contribute in some small way to that cause. Let me conclude with some words of the great Canadian ecumenist, Jean M. R. Tillard, "The time has come, and the situation demands, that the churches should act on the basis that what unites them (or is supposed to continue to unite them) is stronger than what divides them."[4]

---

4. Ibid., 196.

Bibliography

Abraham, William J. *Shaking Hands with the Devil: The Intersection of Terrorism and Theology*. Dallas: Highland Loch, 2013.

Alberigo, Giuseppe. *A Brief History of Vatican II*. Maryknoll, NY: Orbis, 2006.

Anderson, Stafford, et al., eds. *The One Mediator, the Saints, and Mary: Lutherans and Catholics in Dialogue VIII*. Minneapolis: Augsburg Fortress, 1992.

Avis, Paul. *The Identity of Anglicanism*. London: T. & T. Clark, 2007.

Bolan, Donald, and Gregory Cameron, eds. *Mary, Grace and Hope in Christ: The Seattle Statement of the Anglican-Roman Catholic International Commission*. New York: Continuum, 2006.

Butler, Christopher. "Roman Requirements." *The Tablet*, July 5, 1975, 99–100.

Butler, David. *Methodists and Papists: John Wesley and the Catholic Church in the Eighteenth Century*. London: Darton, Longman and Todd, 1995.

Conway, Eamonn. "The Papacy in a Pilgrim Church: Response to Prof. John Macquarrie." In *On Being a Theologian*, by John Macquarrie, 173–77. London: SCM, 1999.

Cummings, Owen F. *Eucharistic Doctors*. Mahwah, NJ: Paulist, 2005.

———. *A History of the Popes in the Twentieth Century*. Lewiston, ME: Mellen, 2008.

———. *John Macquarrie, A Master of Theology*. Mahwah, NJ: Paulist, 2002.

———. *Liturgical Snapshots: Reflections on the Richness of Our Worship Tradition*. Mahwah, NJ: Paulist, 2012.

———. *Prophets, Guardians and Saints*. Mahwah, NJ: Paulist, 2007.

———. *The Theology of John Macquarrie (1919–2007): A Comprehensive and Contextual Exploration*. Lewiston, ME: Mellen, 2010.

———. "Toward a Postliberal Religious Education." *The Living Light* 28 (1992) 315–24.

de Lubac, SJ, Henri. *Catholicism*. Reprint. San Francisco: Ignatius, 1988.

———. *Corpus Mysticum: The Eucharist and the Church in the Middle Ages*. Notre Dame: University of Notre Dame Press, 2006.

———. *The Splendor of the Church*. Reprint. San Francisco: Ignatius, 1999.

Doyle, Dennis. *Communion Ecclesiology*. Maryknoll, NY: Orbis, 2000.

Duffy, Eamon. *Saints and Sinners*. Rev. ed. New Haven: Yale University Press, 2006.

Dulles, SJ, Avery. *The Catholicity of the Church*. Oxford: Clarendon, 1985.

———. *A Church To Believe In*. New York: Crossroad, 1982.

———. "The Decree on Ecumenism: Twenty-five Years After." In *Walking Together: Roman Catholics and Ecumenism Twenty-five Years after Vatican II*, edited by Thaddeus D. Horgan, 17–25. Grand Rapids: Eerdmans, 1990.

———. *Models of the Church*. Rev. ed. Garden City, NY: Doubleday, 2002.

———. *The Resilient Church*. Garden City, NY: Doubleday, 1977.
Empey, Adrian. Foreword to *Healing and Hope*, by Michael Hurley, SJ, 14–15. Dublin: Columba, 2003.
Fagan, SM, Sean. "Theology in the Making." In *Theology in the Making*, edited by Gesa E. Theissen and Declan Marmion, SM, 69–78. Dublin: Veritas, 2005.
Faggioli, Massimo. *Vatican II, the Battle for Meaning*. Mahwah, NJ: Paulist, 2012.
Fahey, SJ, Michael. "Ecumenical Ecclesiology." In *The Gift of the Church*, edited by Peter C. Phan, 111–27. Collegeville, MN: Liturgical, 2000.
Falardeau, SSS, Ernest. "The Eucharistic Challenge to the Churches." *Emmanuel* 119 (2013) 196–205.
Ford, David F. Foreword to *The Irish School of Ecumenics (1970–2007)*, edited by Michael Hurley, SJ, 15–26. Dublin: Columba, 2008.
———. "Wilderness Wisdom for the Twenty-first Century." In *Wilderness, Essays in Honor of Frances Young*, edited by R. S. Sugirtharajah, 153–66. London: T. & T. Clark, 2005.
Forte, Bruno. *The Essence of Christianity*. Grand Rapids: Eerdmans, 2003.
Frend, William H. C. *From Dogma to History*. London: SCM, 2003.
Fuellenbach, SVD, John. *Church, Community for the Kingdom*. Maryknoll, NY: Orbis, 2002.
Gaillardetz, Richard R., and Catherine E. Clifford. *Keys to the Council: Unlocking the Teaching of Vatican II*. Collegeville, MN: Liturgical, 2012.
Gaillardetz, Richard R. "Conversation Starters: Dialogue and Debate during Vatican II." *America*, February 13, 2012, 14–18.
———. "What Can We Learn from Vatican II?" In *The Catholic Church in the Twentieth Century*, edited by Michael J. Himes, 91–100. Liguori, MO: Liguori, 2004.
Hales, Edward E. Y. *Pope John and His Revolution*. Garden City, NY: Doubleday, 1965.
Hanson, A. T., and R. P. C. *The Identity of the Church*. London: SCM, 1987.
Hardy, Daniel W. *Finding the Church: The Dynamic Truth of Anglicanism*. London: SCM, 2001.
———. "John Macquarrie's Ecclesiology." In *In Search of Humanity and Deity: A Celebration of John Macquarrie's Theology*, edited by Robert Morgan, 267–76. London: SCM, 2006.
Hebblethwaite, Peter. *John XXIII, Pope of the Century*. Rev. ed. New York: Continuum, 2000.
Horgan, Thaddeus D., ed. *Walking Together: Roman Catholics and Ecumenism Twenty-five Years after Vatican II*. Grand Rapids: Eerdmans, 1990.
Hunsinger, George. *The Eucharist and Ecumenism*. Cambridge: Cambridge University Press, 2008.
Hurley, SJ, Michael. *Christian Unity: An Ecumenical Second Spring?* Dublin: Veritas, 1998.
———. *Healing and Hope*. Dublin: Columba, 2003.
———, ed. *Irish Anglicanism 1869–1969*. Dublin: Allen Figgis, 1970.
———, ed. *The Irish School of Ecumenics (1970–2007)*. Dublin: Columba, 2008.
———, ed. *John Wesley's Letter to a Roman Catholic*. Nashville: Abingdon, 1968.
———. *Scriptura Sola, Wyclif and His Critics*. New York: Fordham University Press, 1960.
———. *Theology of Ecumenism*. Notre Dame, IN: Fides, 1969.
———. *Towards Christian Unity: An Introduction to the Ecumenical Movement*. Dublin: Veritas, 1961.
John XXIII, Pope. *Journal of a Soul*. Rev. ed. London: Chapman, 1980.

Bibliography

Kärkkäinnen, Veli-Matti. *An Introduction to Ecclesiology*. Downers Grove, IL: InterVarsity, 2002.

Kasper, Walter. "Present Situation and Future of the Ecumenical Movement." *Information Service* (Pontifical Council for Promoting Christian Unity) 109 (2002) 11–20.

———. *That They May All Be One*. New York: Continuum, 2005.

Knox, John. *The Church and the Reality of Christ*. New York: Harper and Row, 1962.

Komonchak, Joseph. "Many Models, One Church." *Church* (Spring 1993) 12–15.

Küng, Hans, ed. *Post-Ecumenical Christianity*. New York: Herder and Herder, 1970.

Lash, Nicholas. *Theology for Pilgrims*. London: Darton, Longman and Todd, 2008.

———. *Voices of Authority*. London: Sheed and Ward, 1976.

Lazareth, William H. "Response to Avery Dulles." In *Walking Together: Roman Catholics and Ecumenism Twenty-five Years after Vatican II*, edited by Thaddeus D. Horgan, 26–32. Grand Rapids: Eerdmans, 1990.

Lindbeck, George. *The Church in a Postliberal Age*. London: SCM, 2002.

———. *The Nature of Doctrine*. London: SPCK, 1984.

Lyons, OSB, Patrick F. "Healing and Hope: Remembering Michael Hurley." *One in Christ* 45 (2011) 260–79.

Macquarrie, John. *Christian Unity and Christian Diversity*. London: SCM, 1975.

———. Foreword to *Rome and Canterbury*, by Mary Reath, vii–viii. Lanham, MD: Rowman and Littlefield, 2007.

———. *On Being a Theologian, Reflections at Eighty*. London: SCM, 1999.

———. *Principles of Christian Theology*. Rev. ed. London: SCM, 1977.

———. "Structures of Unity." In *Their Lord and Ours: Approaches to Authority, Community and the Unity of the Church*, edited by Mark Santer, 33–52, London: SPCK, 1982.

———. *Theology, Church and Ministry*. London: SCM, 1986.

Martini, SJ, Carlo M. *Reflections on the Church*. Dublin: Veritas, 1987.

Massa, SJ, Mark. "A Model Theologian: The Legacy of Avery Dulles." *Commonwealth*, August 13, 2010, 12–16.

McBrien, Richard P. *Catholicism*. London: Chapman, 1984.

McIntosh, Mark. "Christ the Word Who Makes Us: Eucharist and Creation." *Pro Ecclesia* 19 (2010) 255–59.

McPartlan, Paul. *Sacrament of Salvation*. Edinburgh: T. & T. Clark, 1995.

Miller, J. Michael. *The Divine Right of the Papacy in Recent Ecumenical Theology*. Rome: Gregorian University Press, 1980.

Minear, Paul. *Images of the Church in the New Testament*. Louisville: Westminster-John Knox, 1960.

Morris, Jeremy, and Nicholas Sagovsky, eds. *The Unity We Have and the Unity We Seek*. London: T. & T. Clark, 2003.

Murray, Paul D. "Receptive Ecumenism and Catholic Learning—Establishing the Agenda." In *Receptive Ecumenism and the Call to Catholic Learning: Exploring a Way for Contemporary Ecumenism*, edited by Paul D. Murray, 5–25. Oxford: Oxford University Press, 2008.

Newbigin, Lesslie. "All in One Place or All of One Sort? On Unity and Diversity in the Church." In *Creation, Christ and Culture*, edited by Richard W. A. McKinney, 288–306. Edinburgh: T. & T. Clark, 1976.

———. *The Household of God*. New York: Friendship, 1954.

———. "Missions." In *The Concise Encyclopedia of Preaching*, edited by William H. Willimon and Richard Lischer, 335–36. Louisville: Westminster-John Knox, 1995.

Bibliography

Nichols, OP, Aidan. *Engaging Theologians*. Milwaukee,WI: Marquette University Press, 2013.

———. *Epiphany, A Theological Introduction to Catholicism*. Collegeville, MN: Liturgical, 1996.

———. *Figuring Out the Church, Her Marks, and Her Masters*. San Francisco: Ignatius, 2013.

O'Gara, Margaret. "Toward the Day When We Will Keep the Feast Together." *Pro Ecclesia* 19 (2010) 260–66.

O'Malley, SJ, John W. Introduction to *Vatican II: Did Anything Happen?*, edited by David G. Schultenover, 52–91, New York: Continuum, 2007.

Outler, Albert C., ed. *John Wesley*. Oxford: Oxford University Press, 1964.

Radcliffe, OP, Timothy. *What Is the Point of Being a Christian?* New York: Continuum, 2005.

Rafferty, SJ, Oliver. Introduction to *Reconciliation, Essays in Honour of Michael Hurley*, by Oliver Rafferty, SJ, 9–16. Dublin: Columba, 1993.

———, ed. *Reconciliation, Essays in Honour of Michael Hurley*. Dublin: Columba, 1993.

Rahner, SJ, Karl. "A Basic Theological Interpretation of the Second Vatican Council." In *Theological Investigations*, vol. 20, 77–89, New York: Crossroad, 1981.

Robeck, Jr., Cecil. "The Holy Spirit and the Unity of the Church: The Challenge of Pentecostal, Charismatic, and Independent Movements." In *The Holy Spirit, The Church and Christian Unity*, edited by D. Donnelly et al., 358–69. Leuven: Peeters, 2005.

Santer, Mark. "Communion, Unity and Primacy: An Anglican Response to *Ut Unum Sint*," *Ecclesiology* 3 (2007) 283–95.

Schillebeeckx, OP, Edward. *Christ the Sacrament*. Reprint. London: Sheed and Ward, 1987.

Schloesser, SJ, Stephen. "Against Forgetting: Memory, History, Vatican II." In *Vatican II: Did Anything Happen?*, edited by David G. Schultenover, 92–152. New York: Continuum, 2007.

Semmelroth, Otto. *Church and Sacrament*. Notre Dame, IN: Fides, 1965.

Shannon, David T. "A Free Church Perspective on the Decree and Ecumenism." In *Walking Together: Roman Catholics and Ecumenism Twenty-five Years after Vatican II*, edited by Thaddeus D. Horgan, 33–58. Grand Rapids: Eerdmans, 1990.

Suenens, Léon-Joseph. *Memories and Hopes*. Dublin: Veritas, 1992.

———. "A Plan for the Whole Council." In *Vatican II by Those Who Were There*, edited by Alberic Stacpoole, OSB, 88–91. London: Chapman, 1985.

Sumner, George. "After Dromantine." *Anglican Theological Review* 87 (2005) 559–66.

Tanner, Mary. "Towards Visible Unity." In *Reconciliation, Essays in Honor of Michael Hurley*, edited by Oliver Rafferty, SJ, 18–31. Dublin: Columba, 1993.

Tanner, SJ, Norman P., ed. *Decrees of the Ecumenical Councils*. 2 vols. Washington, DC: Georgetown University Press, 1990.

Tavard, George H. *Two Centuries of Ecumenism*. Notre Dame, IN: Fides, 1962.

Theisen, OSB, Jerome P. *The Ultimate Church and the Promise of Salvation*. Collegeville, MN: St. John's University Press, 1976.

Tillard, OP, Jean M. R. *Church of Churches*. Collegeville, MN: Liturgical, 1992.

———. "*Ex Tenebris Lux*: Ecumenism Enters a New Phase." In *The Unity We Have and the Unity We Seek*, edited by Jeremy Morris et al., 191–202. : T. & T. Clark, 2003.

Bibliography

———. *I Believe, Despite Everything: Reflections of an Ecumenist.* Collegeville, MN: Liturgical, 2003.
Tobin, John, ed. *George Herbert, The Complete English Poems.* London: Penguin, 1991.
Tracy, David. *The Analogical Imagination.* London: SCM, 1981.
———. *Blessed Rage for Order.* Rev. ed. Chicago: University of Chicago Press, 1996.
Trevor, Meriol. *Pope John.* Garden City, NY: Doubleday, 1968.
Vogel, Arthur A. "The Decree on Ecumenism and the Challenge of the Future." In *Walking Together: Roman Catholics and Ecumenism Twenty-five Years after Vatican II*, edited by Thaddeus D. Horgan, 1–10. Grand Rapids: Eerdmans, 1990.
Vokes, Frederick E. *The Riddle of the Didache.* London: SPCK, 1938.
Wainwright, Geoffrey. "Catholics and Methodists in Conversation: A Progress Report (1991–2006)." *Milltown Studies* 53 (2004) 38–71.
———. *Doxology, A Systematic Theology.* Oxford: Oxford University Press, 1984.
———. *The Ecumenical Moment: Crisis and Opportunity for the Church.* Grand Rapids: Eerdmans, 1983.
———. *Embracing Purpose: Essays on God, the World and the Church.* London: Epworth, 2007.
———. *Is the Reformation Over?* Milwaukee, WI: Marquette University Press, 2000.
———. *Lesslie Newbigin: A Theological Life.* New York: Oxford University Press, 2000.
———. *Methodists in Dialogue.* Nashville: Kingswood/Abingdon, 1995.
———. "Roman Catholic-Methodist Dialogue: A Silver Jubilee." In *Reconciliation, Essays in Honour of Michael Hurley*, edited by Oliver Rafferty, SJ, 53–79. Dublin: Columba, 1993.
Wicks, SJ, Jared. "The Significance of the 'Ecclesial Communities' of the Reformation." *Ecumenical Trends* 30 (December 2001) 10–13.
———. "Six Texts by Professor Joseph Ratzinger." *Gregorianum* 89 (2008) 233–311.
Williams, Rowan D. "Profile: Frances Young." In *Wilderness, Essays in Honor of Frances Young*, edited by R. S. Sugirtharajah, 1–7. London: T. & T. Clark, 2005.
Wood, Susan. "The Theology of Communion as and Ecumenical Resource." In *Walking Together: Roman Catholics and Ecumenism Twenty-five Years after Vatican II*, edited by Thaddeus D. Horgan, 103–10. Grand Rapids: Eerdmans, 1990.
World Council of Churches. *Baptism, Eucharist and Ministry.* Faith and Order Paper, no. 111. Geneva: World Council of Churches, 1982.
———. *The Nature and Purpose of the Church.* Faith and Order Paper, no. 181. Bialystok, Poland: Ortdruck Orthodox, 1998.
Young, Frances M., and Kenneth Wilson. *Focus on God.* London: Epworth, 1986.
Young, Frances M. *The Art of Performance: Towards a Theology of Holy Scripture.* London: Darton, Longman and Todd, 1990.
———. *Brokenness and Blessing: Towards a Biblical Spirituality.* London: Darton, Longman and Todd, 2007.
———. *Can These Dry Bones Live?* Rev. ed. London: SCM, 1992.
———, ed. *Dare We Speak of God in Public?* London: Mowbray, 1995.
———, ed. *Encounter with Mystery: Reflections on L'Arche and Living with Disability.* London: Darton, Longman and Todd, 1997.
———. "The Great Thanksgiving Prayer." In *Living the Eucharist*, edited by Stephen Conway, 79–94. London: Darton, Longman and Todd, 2001.

Bibliography

———. "Theotokos: Mary and the Pattern of Fall and Redemption in the Theology of Cyril of Alexandria." In *Mary for Earth and Heaven*, edited by William McLoughlin et al., 314–54. Leominster, UK: Gracewing, 2002.

Zizioulas, John D. *Being as Communion, Studies in Personhood and the Church*. London: Darton, Longman and Todd, 1985.

———. "The Eucharist and the Kingdom of God, Part 3." *Sourozh* 60 (1995) 32–46.

www.ingramcontent.com/pod-product-compliance
Lightning Source LLC
Chambersburg PA
CBHW071450160426

43195CB00013B/2074